Acholi Dictionary -English

Africa
World Books
Pty Ltd

Contents

Foreword

This dictionary is published without any funding or assistance from any source. I published this dictionary through the Ongee Foundation, *Gang kwan me Acholi*. It is money I earned personally from work as an interpreter which has enabled me to write this book under the name of my business.

As a language Acholi is used in business, culture, telecommunications and travel.

Acholi is spoken in Uganda and South Sudan. Small numbers of Acholi people migrated to Australia, USA, Canada, New Zealand, UK, Europe and Scandinavia and some of the older people who settled in those countries still practise the language. Because of the activities of the Lord's Resistance Army, who, for some time, have terrorised the Ugandan civilian population, the Acholi language has been used in the International Tribunal Court to try those who have committed human rights abuses against civilians in Northern Uganda.

This dictionary is intended for those who are already fluent in speaking and writing Acholi. If you do not feel you are advanced in speaking and writing the Acholi language then you should use an Acholi beginner dictionary rather than this one.

English words are rich in figurative language and I have attempted to provide the equivalent phrase in Acholi (as well as supplying the literal meaning).

Due to funding restrictions I have not been able to employ a peer editor and so have decided not to use phonetic characters and accents. Unfortunately, this includes those words which have the same spelling but can only be distinguished by the accents. With increased funding I hope to rectify this is in future editions.

I finished High school in Kakuma Refugee Camp, Kenya and from therew migrated to Australia in 2006. In Kakuma, I worked as a Deputy Head Master in a primary school and a volunteer editor for the *Kakuma News Bulletin*. In Australia I graduated from the University of Adelaide in 2010 with a Bachelor of Media degree with Honours.

I have worked with several companies in Australia as an interpreter working on-site, over the telephone and also in the detention centres in Papua New Guinea and Nauru employed by the Department of Immigration and Border Protection.

Please enjoy your reading or studying. Your feedback is welcome at tabanongee@outlook.com.

Abbreviation

Adj. Adjective

Adv. adverb

n. Noun

lit. Literarily

v. Verb

n. leg. Noun as a legal term

Note on the entries

1. I have not employed the use of phonology sound to distinguish the tone language at this time, but I hope to use it in the future as there is no funding for such project.

2. The tone languages are written the same but it required phonetic marked to distinguish what the person actual mean. In future, if there is funding, such phonetic marked and stress is important to emphasis what the speaker actually mean.

3. **Awobi** (*n*): boy,

> The abbreviation in the italic is used to indicate that the word provided is a noun. verbs etc.

4. **Bolo** (ki anyot) (*v*): dump

> Those words put in the brackets are used to emphasise the meaning of the given words in Acholi. The speaker can choose to use the word with a combination of the given word or vocabulary in order to give a clear meaning.

Acholi Basic Grammar

Acholi Alphabet

Acholi alphabet though written similarly to English alphabet, it is quite different to English alphabet. One needs to put more effort in order to read Acholi alphabet. The following below is Acholi alphabet.

A	B	C	D
E	F	G	H
I	J	K	L
M	N	O	P
R	S	T	U
V	W	Y	

<u>Pronounciation of the Alphabet</u>

Acholi has no alphabet Q, X and Z. Due to mother tongue interference; Acholi cannot pronounce the letter Q, X and Z. This mother toungue interference do not afftect people who come into contact with other languages other than Acholi. As a linguist, our focus is what a typical Acholi can pronounce is all what we can produce to you as an alphabet. This is drawing to the work of ther previous work of linguist in Acholi who wrote Bible and other literature such as hymn song in Acholi language.

How Acholi pronounce their alphabet as given in the following list below. Acholi pronounce:

A as /a/ as in <u>a</u>pple

B as /b/ as in <u>b</u>all

C as /c/ as in <u>c</u>hart

D as /d/ as in <u>d</u>ad

E as /e/ as in <u>e</u>ggs

F as /f/ as in <u>f</u>at. However, Acholi normally replaced the alphabet /F/ with /P/. That is to say the phonetic /f/ does not exist in Acholi , and if it exist is not common.

H as /h/ as in <u>h</u>at. Nevertheless, Acholi do not use /h/ in their speech. Instead of /h/, they use A in their speech.

I as /i/ as in ink

J as /j/ as in jug

K as /k/ as in Karl

L as /l/ as in last

M as /m/ as in mad

N as /n/ as in nap

O as /o/ as in open

P as /p/ as in paper

R as /r/ as in rat

S as /s/ as in sad. However, Acholi do not have phonetic /s/ because they replaced phonetic /s/ with /c/. As a result the pronunciations of the phonetic /s/ is quiet difficult for the Acholi speakers.

T as /t/ as in tug

U as /u/ as in book

V as /v/ as in vast. Conversely, Acholi do not use the alphabet /v/ in their speech since /v/ is replaced with phonetic /b/.

W as /w/ as in warm

Y as /y/ as in yard

Some other Acholi alphabet sound – we approximate the sound as it is difficult to find in English but it require future linguistic study

By as close as /bia/ which is almost close to beer [biə]

Dy as close as /dia/ which is practically close to dear [diə]

Gw as close as as /gu:/ which is virtually close to gourlash ['gu:læʃ]

Ly as close to /lia/ which is basically close to laison [li'eizn]

My as close as /mia/ which is practically close to meander [mi'ændə]

Ng /ŋ/ as in looking

Ny as close as to/nia/ which is almost close to near [niə]

Py as close as to /pia/ which is roughly close to piano [pi'ænəu]

Ry as close as to /ria/ which is virtually close to realize [ri: əlaiz]

Ty as close as to /tie/ which is basically close to tear [teə]

Acholi consonant

B	C	D	F
G	H	J	K
L	M	N	P
R	S	T	V
W	Y		

Acholi Vowel

A	E	I	O	U

Acholi sound

The combination of the consonants and vowels make the Acholi sound. For example, B + A sound as ba as in bar. The below list of- show how the combination of vowel and consonant make sound in Acholi.

B + a =Ba

C + e =Ce

P +u = Pu

Acholi syllable

The combinations of sound form a syllable.

Ba	Be	Bi	Bo	Bu
Ca	Ce	Ci	Co	Cu

Da	De	Di	Do	Du
Fa	Fe	Fi	Fo	Fu
Gi	Ge	Gi	Go	Gu
Ha	He	Hi	Ho	Hu
Ja	Je	Ji	Jo	Ju
Ka	Ke	Ki	ko	Ku
La	Le	Li	Lo	Lu
Ma	Me	Mi	Mo	Mu
Na	Ne	Ni	No	Nu
Pa	Pe	Pi	Po	Pu
Ra	Re	Ri	Ro	Ru
Sa	Se	Si	So	Su
Ta	Te	Ti	To	Tu
Va	Ve	Vi	Vo	Vu
Wa	We	Wi	Wo	Wu
Ya	Ye	Yi	Yo	Yu
Bya	Bye	Byi	Byo	Byu
Dya	Dye	Dyi	Dyo	Dyu
Gwa	Gwe	Gwi	Gwo	Gwu
Lya	Lye	Lyi	Lyo	Lyu
Mya	Mye	Myi	Myo	Myu
Pya	Pye	Pyi	Pyo	Pyu
Rya	Rye	Ryi	Ryo	Ryu
Tya	Tye	Tyi	Tyo	Tyu

If you know how to read the combination of the sylable above, it will be easy to read Acholi. Forexample if you add one syllable and another syllable it will make a meaningful word:

Ba + ba = Baba
   (father)

Ka + ka = kaka
   (tribe)

A+nya + ka =Anyaka
    (a girl)

Grammar

Word order

The word order in Acholi follows the frequent pattern of Subject + verb + object which is equivalent to English word order parttern.

Article

Acholi has no indefite article such as a and an. However, it has a definite article the (ne) at the end of word.

Boy	Awobi	The boy	Awobi ne
Girl	Anyaka	The girl	Anyaka ne
Rain	kot	The rain	Kot ne
Snake	Twol	The snake	Twol ne

Plural

Acholi plural is made up of regular and irregular noun. Some of the plural you have to learn it.

1. **Regular plural**

   There are three type of regular plural in Acholi. These plural are:

   a. Regular plural comprised of article ne and word gini coming at the end of subject.

Cassava	Gwana	Cassavas	Gwana ne gini
Bottle	Cupa	Bottles	Cupa ne gini
Book	Buk	Books	Buk ne gini
Shoe	war	Shoes	War ne gini
Picture	Cal	Pictures	Cal ne gini

   b. The second regular plural is when a suffix at the end of the subject changes and replaces or added with i. Example of these type of plural are:

Chair	Kom	Chairs	Komi
Goat	Dyel	Goats	Dyegi
Sheep	Romo	Sheep	Romi

c. The third plural is a matter of changing a prefix La to Lo in order to make a plural.

Child	Latin	Children	Lotino
Parent	Lanyodo	Parents	Lonyodo

2. Irregular plural

There are as many of irregular plural in Acholi that you have to learn it by heart. The following few exampleof irregular plural in Acholi that you have learn by heart. These are:

Boy	Awobi	Boys	Awobe
Girl	Anyaka	Girls	Anyira
Woman	Dako	Women	Mon

Adjective

Adjective come after the noun and the pronoun they describe. It comes after the subject inorder to define, qualified and quantified noun and pronoun.

The big dog	Gwoke ne dit
	(*lit*. Dog the big)

The book is cheap	Buk ne yot
	(*lit*. Book the cheap)

Plural- adjective

The adjective plural is made out of third person plural gi (they) and the the derivative o coming at the suffix of the adjective describing the noun or pronoun. Sometimes the derivative o is omitted in speech at the suffix of the adjective that describing the subject. Gi (they) sometimes are pronounce gu, it depend with the speaker about which one is easier or difficult for him or her.

The boy is bad	Awobi ne rac	The boys are bads	Awobe ne gi raco
	(lit. Boy the bad)		(lit. Boys the bads)
The chair is broken	Kom ne otur	The chairs are broken	Komi ne gi tur
	(lit. chair the it broke/en)		(lit. Chairs the they broken)
The bottle is broken	Cupa ne otyer	The bottles are broken	Cupa ne gini gi tyer
	(lit. Bottle the it broke)		(lit. bottles they broken)

The shoe is torn	War ne oyec	The shoes are torn	War ne gini gi yec
	(lit. shoes the it torn)		(lit. shoes they broken)

Comparative and Superlative adjective

Comparative adjective has to include the word loyo which mean defeat, victory or better than in the main adjective in order to form comparative adjective while with superlative adjective you have to incorporate loyo and the word weŋ which mean all at the end of the main adjective inorder to form superlative adjective.

Adjective		Comprative adjective		Superlative adjective	
Good	Ber	Better	Ber loyo	Best	Ber loyo weŋ
Big	Dit	Bigger	Dit loyo	Biggest	Dit loyo weŋ
Cheap	Yot	Cheaper	Yot loyo	Cheapest	Yot loyo weŋ

Demostratives

There are two types of demonstrative pronoun in Acholi language.

Singulara		Plural	

With this type of demonstrative, morpheme ni preside the demonstrative to mean one.

This	En ni	These	Eno ni
That	Caa ni	Those	Cage ni

This medicine is bitter	Yat eni kec
	(lit. medicine this one bitter)

Those men	Coo eno ni
	(lit. Men those one)

or

Singulara		Plural	
This	Man	These	munu
That	maka	Those	Mugu

Buk man ipara

Galam maka peri

Komi munu ituwa

Cale ne gini mugu ituwa

n   n

n

en

An		wan
In		wun
En		Gin

An a mito cito diki

A mito cito diki

Gin gi tero buk ne laworo

Gi tero buk ne laworo

En cito diki

She is going tomorrow	Cito diki
	(lit. Go tomorrow)
He closed the door	En opuŋo dogolo
	(lit. he closed door)
He closed the door	Opuŋo dogolo
	(lit. closed door)

Objective pronun

The objective pronoun is equal to the subject pronoun with exception of adding t to singular objective pronouns such as " ta'', me and deletion of n from the suffix of plural of objective pronouns such as "wu" us.

Singular		*plural*	
Me	an/ta	Us	Wan/wa
You	in/ti	You	Wun/ wu
Him, her, it	en/te	Them	Gin/gi

You come to me	Bin bota
	(lit.Come to me)
They give it to you	Gi miyo boti
	(lit. They give to you)
They fought me	Gi lwenyo i kom an
	(lit. They fought in body me)
They beat them	Gi goyo gin
	(lit. They beat them)
He stole us	Okwalo wan
	(lit. Stole us)
You cheat him	I bwolo en
	(lit . You cheat him)

<u>Verb</u>

There are two main tense in Acholi Language. The present tense and the past tense verbs is the one use in all the tenses. The other tenses like the past perfect tense and the future tense are also use but their verbs is also similar to the verbs uses in the main tenses. For example, the future tense verb is similar to the present tense verb and the past perfect tense verb is similar to the past tense verb.

Present tense

Although you do not need to put o as a suffix or at the end of the present tense verb, sometime you have to use it in speech or writing.

Shut	Puŋ
Run	Riŋ
Look	Nen
Run there	Wu riŋ kuca
Shut it out	Gi puŋ woko
He comes here everday	En riŋo kany nino ducu
He looks there everday	En neno kuca jwijwi

Future tense

Similar to present tense, sometimes you have to put o as a suffix or at the end of verb of future tense in your speech or writing.

Buy	wil
Wash	lwok
Call	lwoŋ
You call him tomorrow	Wu lwoŋ en diki
She will buy tomorrow	En wilo diki
She will call tomorrow	En lwoŋo diki

Past tense

Past tense has o as a prefix and o as a suffix at the given verb. To sound better, you have to ignore pronoun at the beginning of the clause or sentence.

Drank	Omato
Played	Otuko

Sat	Obedo
He drank yesterday	En omato laworo (lit. He drank yesterday)
He drank yesterday	Omato laworo (lit. Drank yesterday)
He played yesterday	En otuko laworo (lit. He played yesterday)
He played yesterday	Otuko laworo (lit. Played yesterday)

Past perfect tense

Likewise, Past tense, past perfect tense has o as a prefix and o as a suffix at the given verb. Again to sound better, you have to ignore pronoun at the beginning of the clause or sentence.

Come	Obino
Gone	Ocito
Eaten	Ocamo
He has just come now	En obino pudi koni (lit. He comes just now)
He has just come now	Obino pudi koni (lit. Come just now)
He has just gone now	En ocito pudi koni (lit. He gone just now)
He has just gone now	Ocito pudi koni (lit. Gone just now)

<u>The verb to be</u>

Present tense

As people speak fast, they tend to delete the pronoun as a subject in the beginning of the clause or sentence.

I am	An a	We are	Wan wa

You are	In i	You are	wun wu
He/She/It is	En e	They are	Gin gi

I am going tomorrow	A cito diki
	(lit. I going tomorrow)

They are tired	Gi der
	(lit. They tired)

Past tense

Just a reminder again, as people speak fast, they tend to ignore the pronoun as a subject in the beginning of the clause or sentence.

I was	An a	we were	Wan wa
You were	In i	You were	wun wu
He/She/It was	En e	They were	Gin gi

They were drinking alcohol yesterday	Gin gi mato koŋo laworo
	(lit. They they were drinking alcohol yesterday)

They were drinking alcohol yesterday	Gi mato koŋo laworo
	(lit. They were drinking alcohol yesterday)

I was fighting them last week	An a lwenyo ki gin i cabit mukato
	(lit. I was fighting with them in week pass)

I was fighting them last week	A lwenyo ki gin i cabit mukato
	(lit. I was fighting with them in week pass)

Past perfect tense

The same things like the rest of the verb to be, as people speak fast, they tend to ignore the pronoun as a subject in the beginning of the clause or sentence.

I have	an a	we have	Wan wa
You have	In i	You have	wun wu
He/She/It has	En e	They have	Gin gi

I have read the book	A kwano buk ne
	lit. I read book the)

He has read the newspaper	Okwano lok aŋeya ne
	(lit. he has read newpaper)
We have taken the body home	Wa tero kome ne gaŋ
	(lit. we took body the home)
They have beaten him	Gi goyo en
	(lit. They beat him)
You have bought the patato	I wilo liyata ne
	(lit. You bought patato the)

Modals

I can	A twero
You can	I twero
They can	Gi twero
He can	En twero

Want

I want	A mito
He wants	En mito

Must/Have to/ need to

An obligation modal such as must comes after the clause or sentence as given in the example below.

I must go	Myero a citi
	(lit. must I go)
We must go	Myero wa citi
	(lit. must we go)

Possesion

My	ipara	Ours	ituwa

Your	I peri	Yours	I tuu
His/her/its	I pere	Theirs	I tugi

The possessor comes after the subject it possessed.

My book	Buk para
	(lit. Book mine)
Your book	Buk peri
	(lit. Book your)
Our book	Buk tuwa
	(lit. Book ours)
Her book	Buk pere
	(lit. Book his)
Yours book	Buk tuu
	(lit. Book yours)
Their book	Buk tugi
	(lit. Book their)

Questions

When?	Awene?
Why?	Piŋo?
Where?	Kany?
What?	Ngo?
How	Niniŋ?
Who	Nga?
Which	Man?

Questions can be formed by changing statement such as raising flat intonation to high intonation

He brought the pen	En okelo galam ne
Did he bring the pen?	Okelo galam ne?
	(lit. he bring pen the?)

Interogation question can be placed at the end of the sentence and sometime can be place at the beginning of the sentence for emphasis.

Where is the party?	Ayub ne tye kany?
	(lit. party the is where?)
	Kany ayub ne?
	(lit. where party the)

Negatives

The prefix pe and suffix ko are used in the negative statement.

He did	Otimo
He did not	Otimo ko
She cried	Okok
She did not cried	Pe okok

Conjuction

Because	Pi tyen lok eni
For	bot
And	Ki
Yet	pudi
So	pi eni
But	Ento
Or	Nyo
If	Ka
Until	wakoni
Since	wacon
Than	loyo
John and Mary	John gin ki Mary

(lit. John they and Mary)

I or you   An nyo in

(I or you)

Acholi – English Dictionary

A

A jiji (*adj*): traumatic, shocked,

A juk pa kot i coc (*n, leg.*): writ,

A luŋ tuke (*adv*): upside-down,

Aa ma ger (*v*): explode,

Aa woko (kikenyo) (*v*): stay, step,

Abak (*adj*): assured, guarantee,

Abak (*n*): pledge, security,

Abak (*n*): quotation, estimate,

Abara wic (*n*): headache,

Abara wic ma waŋo wic (*n*): migraine,

Aber (*adj*): ironic, sarcastic,

Abic (*n*): five,

Abicel (*n*): six,

Abil (*n*): taste,

Abili (*n*): police,

Abiro (*n*): seven,

Abiulanc (*n*): Ambulance,

Aboma (*adj*): sly, deceitful, crafty, cunning, devious,

Aboŋwen (*n*): nine,

Abor (*n*): lung,

Aboro (*n*): eigth,

Abutida (*adj*): elastic,

Abwoli ko (*adj*): guarantee, certain, assured, (*lit.*)I am not lying, confident,

Abyero (*n*): bladder,

Acac (*adj*): numerous, many,

Acaki me neno ne (*adj*): unsual, strange, odd, extraodrdinary, abnormal, remarkable, bizarre,

Acaki podi me neno (*adj*): fantastic, unbelievable,

Acakki (*n*): start, beginning,

Acakki ne ki agiki ne pe (*adj*): immense,

Acam (*n*): left,

Acama (*adj*): edible,

Accaki me gaŋ kwan (*n*): primary school,

Acel (*adj*): single,

Acel (*n*): one,

Acel acel (*adj*): each

Acel keken (*adj*): sole,

Acel me aŋwen (*adj*): quarterly,

Acir (*n*): juice,

Aconya (*adj*): ancient, old fashioned, antique, very old, aged, historic, old –fashioned, obsolete,

Acpirin (*n*): aspirin,

Acut (*n*): vulture,

Acwer (*n*): strut, support,

Acwic (*n*): right,

Acwiny (*n*): liver,

Adaa (*adj*): true, sure, genuine, real, authentic, indisputable, unadulterated, legitimate, valid, actual, certain, guarantee, assured, reliable, dependable realistic, accurate, honest, truthful, sincere, frank, candid, truthful,

Adaa daa (*adv*): really,

Adaa pere pe (*adj*): unrealisitic,

Adane (*adj*): definite,

Adaya (*adj*): bar,

Adaya (*n*): bar,

Adek (*n*): three,

Adoŋ (*n*): slap, hit, knock, bash, blow,

Adot (*n*): report,

Aduno (*adj*): circular, round,

Aduno (*adv*): around,

Aduno (*n*): heart,

Aduno cor cor (*adj*): cylindrical,

Adwala (*n*): flourish,

Agikki (*adj*): last,

Agikki (*n*): finish, close, end,

Agikki (*n*): limit, tip,

Agikki ne (*adj*): ultimate, final,

Agit (*n*): ring,

Aguba (*n*): sip,

Aguragura (*n*): cart,

Agwada (*n*): scratch,

Agweta (*n*): mark, score,

Ajiji (*n*): shock,

Aju (*adj*): draft,

Ajuru (*n*): whirlwind, tornado, hurricane, cyclone,

Ajwaka (*n*): witch doctor,

Aka (*adj*): deliberate, intentional, intentionally, gross, willful,

Aka ko (*adj*): unwitting, unsuspecting, unaware, ignorant, innocent, unintentional, accidental,

Akalakala (*adj*): suspicious, doubtful, questionable, doubt,

Akalakala (*v*): doubt,

Akalakala pe (*adj*): positive, (*lit.*). no doubt,

Akanya ŋo (yubo kom ko) (*adj*): unkempt,

Akara (*adj*): forked,

Akemo (*adj*): wrathful, furious, angry, irate, enraged,

Akemo (*n*): anger, resentment, antagonism, rage,

Akira (*n*): spray,

Akoba (*n*): print,

Akoda (*adj*): humour,

Akoda (*n*): jest, joke, play,

Alii (*n*): stir,

Alii (*n, leg.*): tort,

Alii (*v*): move, provoke,

Alim alim (*n*): sweet,

Aloka aloka (*n*): change, alteration, shift, twist,

Aloko (*n*): hoe,

Alumalum (*adj*): evergreen, green,

Aluŋ (*n*): valley,

Aluŋ tuke (*adj*): wavy,

Aluŋ tuke (*n*): bumb,

Aluu (yamo) (*adj*): gaseous,

Amalo (*v*): rise, wake,

Amama (*n*): monster, ogre, fiend,

Amara (*adj*): adorable, beloved, darling, dear, warm, loving, tender,

Amara (*n*): love, darling, pet, favourite,

Amara maloyo weŋ (*adj*): dearest,

Amerika (*n*): America,

Amut (*n*): exploit,

Amwonya (*adj*): glamorous,

Amyela myela kom (*adj*): snappy, hasty,

An (*pron.*): I, me,

An ki koma (*pron.*): myself,

Angec (*adj*): back, rear, reverse, flipside,

Angec aŋec (*n*) reverse,

Anwoya (*adj*): second –hand, used,

Anyaka (*n*): girl,

Anyim (*adj*): advanced, front, infront,

Anyim (*adv*): forward,

Anyira nyira (*adv*): girlish,

Anyo (*n*): chiken pox,

Anyoba anyoba (*adj*): unruly, disorderly, turbulent,

Anyogi (*n*): maize,

Anywali me gaŋ (*adj*): indigenous, native, aboriginal, home –grown, local and original,

Anywar (*adj*): abuse, assault, giddy, mortified,

Aŋec (*n*): back, rear,

Aŋec aŋec (*adj*): aback,

Aŋec aŋeca (*n*): reverse,

Aŋwen (*n*): four,

Aona (*n*): cough,

Aona opiyo (*n*): tuberculosis,

Aona opiyo ki lyeto marac (*n*): whooping cough,

Apaka (*n*): swampy,

Apar (*n*): ten,

Apar wiye acel (*n*): eleven,

Apir (*adj*): spiteful, malicious,

Apir (*n*): grudge,

Apo pora (*adj*): dramatic,

Apoka apoka (in kin dano) (*adv*): divisive,

Apoka poka me lobo moni matye pi loc pire kene (*n*): state,

Apol (*n*): apple,

Apopora (*n*): play, theatrical production,

Apwoyo (*n*): rabbit, hare,

Araba (*adj*): flat,

Arabiya (*n*): vehicle,

Aranyi (*adj*): criminal,

Arem (*n*): ache, pain, hurt,

Arem ic (*n*): stomached,

Arem it (*n*): earache,

Arem me lak (*n*): toothace,

Arem pa dwan (*n*): sore throat,

Aribariba ma tye kamaleŋ (*adj*): official,

Arii (*adj*): width, horizontal,

Arii arii (*adj*): diagonal,

Ariyo (*n*): two,

Ariyo ariyo (*n*): pair,

Ariyo riyo (*adj*): dual,

Aroma roma (*adj*): accident,

Aruba wic (*adj*): woozy,

Ata (*adj*): random,

Ata ata (*adv*): hapazhard,

Ata ata (*adv*): randomly,

Atako (*n*): appendix,

Atako (*n*): kidney,

Atema tema (*n*): test, trial,

Atir (*adj*): direct, fair, just, frank, honest, genuine, real, authentic, indisputable, true, unadulterated, legitimate, valid, actual, trustworthy, direct, straightforward, candid, right, straight,

Atir (*adv*) upright, just,

Atir (*n*): claim, right,

Atir ko (*adj*): wrong, amiss, not right, incorrect, improper, inappropriate, unsuitable,

Atir ko (*adv*): abnormally,

Atir pere pe (*adj*): phony,

Atire (*n*): point, detail,

Atudu (*n*): duck,

Atum (*adj*): bow,

Atum (*n*): bow,

Atunya (*n*): lion,

Atura (*adj*): unexpected, abrupt, sudden,

Ature (*n*): flower, bloom,

Ature ne tye makwar marmar (*adj*): rosy,

Atutu (*n*): whirlwind, tornado, hurricane, cyclone,

Aura (*adj*): amazing, spectacular, remarkable, visually impressive, unbelievable, dazzling, stunning, astounding,

Auu (*n*): influenza, flu,

Awene (*adv*): when,

Awira awira (*n*): whirl, spin,

Awira wic (*adj*): dizzy, faint, giddy, lightheaded, woozy,

Awira wira wic (*n*): spin,

Awobe awobe (*adv*): boyishly,

Awobi (*n*): boy,

Awobi (opii) (*adj*): knavish,

Awobi awobi (*adv*): knavishly,

Awoo (*adj*): anger, fray,

Awora (*adj*): honorable, adorable, prestigious, respectable, virtuous, inspiring worship or veneration, inspiring great affection or admiration, charming and delightful,

Ayela (*adj*): troubled,

Ayela pe (*adj*): Ok,

Ayela yela pe iye (*adv*): restfully,

Ayila ayila kom (*adj*): snappy, showing impatient, itchy,

Ayila yila kom (miti) (*n*): itch,

Ayub (*n*): party,

B

Bacala (*n*): onion,

Bad (*n*): arm,

Bakacic (*adj*): prize, reward,

Bako (*v*): bid,

Bako (*v*): book,

Bako (*v*): foretell, predict, guess, presume, assume, speculate, surmise,

Bako cat manyen (*n*): venture, new business enterprise,

Bako dog (*n*): supplication, appeal, request,

Bako dog (*n, leg.*): pleadings,

Bako dog (*v*): implore, appeal, groan, plead, beg earnestly,

Bako dog pa ŋat mudoto (me ngeyo gin aŋo ma lular lok otimo) (*n, leg.*): cross appeal,

Bal (*adj*): wrong, immoral, wicked, dishonest, illegal, sinful, iniquitous, criminal, unethical, flaw, mistake, guilty, bad, evil, corrupt, errant, aberrant,

Bal (*n*): damage, ruin,

Bal (*n*): sin, flaw,

Bale oyoto (*adj*): tender, easily damaged,

Baligiti (*n*): blanket,

Balo (nyonyo calo arabiya) (*v*): break,

Balo (*v*): ruin, damage, spoil, mar,

Balo (*v*): sin,

Balo (*v*): waste,

Balo ga (*adj*): wasteful,

Balo ga abala (*adj*): lavish,

Balo ga ko (*adj*): efficiently, not wasteful, economically, cost-effective, ecologically ware,

Balo kido (*adj*): disfigured,

Balo kiji kiji (*v*): wreck,

Balo makwak (*adj*): disastrous,

Balo nyiŋ (*v*): blot,

Balo nyiŋ (*v*): brand,

Balo wic (*v*): harass,

Baŋ (*n*): bank,

Bata (*n*): duck,

Batu (*n*): yam,

Bayo (*v*): miss, fail to spot,

Bayo ŋom (*v*): falter,

Bedi ki adaa (*adj*): realistic, truthful, accurately, faithful, genuine, true, lifelike, convincing,

Bedo (tugi) maber (*adj*) harmonious,

Bedo (*v*): attend,

Bedo (*v*): keep, stay,

Bedo (*v*): live, stay, reside,

Bedo (*v*): sit,

Bedo cal puc (*adj*): feline,

Bedo cal teŋ gaŋ kal (*adj*): suburban,

Bedo calo latin (*adj*): infantile, childish,

Bedo calo pul (*adj*): nutty,

Bedo calo waya (*adj*): wiry,

Bedo doki ceŋ (*adj*) sunny,

Bedo doki kado (*adj*): salty,

Bedo doki kwok (*adj*): sweaty,

Bedo doki moo (*adj*): oily,

Bedo doki nyal (*adj*): rusty,

Bedo doki okutu (*adj*): thorny, prickly,

Bedo doki pii (*adj*): damp,

Bedo doki pii pii (*adj*): moist, humid, damp,

Bedo doki yece (*adj*): feathery,

Bedo doki yer (*adj*): hairy,

Bedo kado kado (*adj*): salty,

Bedo ki kalakala (*v*): question, doubt,

Bedo ki tek wic (*v*): presume, dare, venture,

Bedo kilokilo (*adj*): flaky, detaching, coming off, peeling,

Bedo lemeleme (ibiloga) (*adj*): pungent,

Bedo lewic lewic (*adv*): bashfully,

Bedo maber (*adj*): positive, hopeful,

Bedo macan (*adj*): miserable,

Bedo midmida (*adj*): soggy, clammy, damp,

Bedo mot (*adj*): idle,

Bedo mune mune (*n*): paste,

Bene (*adv*): too,

Benus (*n*): Venus,

Ber (*adj*): good, beneficially, helpfully, usefully, constructively, decent, favourable, advantageous, fine, ideal, suitable, lofty, nice, significant, substantial, siginificant, important, considerate, warm, kindly, well,

Ber (*adj*): kind, angelic,

Ber (i lagam me gi moni) (*adj*): decisive,

Ber (ka kame bedo) (*adj*): hospitable,

Ber (*n*): comfort,

Ber atiŋa (*adj*): cuddly,

Ber do (*adj*): smug,

Ber keket ko (*adj*): worse,

Ber kit (*adj*): unselfish, kind, nice,

Ber kit (*n, leg.*): natural justice,

Ber ko (*adv*): abnormally,

Ber loyo (*adj*): best,

Ber loyo weŋ (*adj*): excellent, great, outstanding, superb, superior, tremendous,

Ber makwak (*adj*): golden, magnificient, superb,

Ber maloyo weŋ (*n*): flower, best

Ber me (*adj*): worthy,

Berber (a*dj*): better,

Berber (*adv*): rightfully, fairly,

Berber mo (*adv*): zestfully,

Berber mo (calo ki myel) (*adj*): colourful,

Bero (*adj*): kind,

Beyo (*v*): allude,

Bibino (*v*): become,

Bibino (*v*): form, cause something to develop,

Bic (*n*): crush,

Bic (*n*): rinse,

Bic (*n*): squash, squeeze,

Bido (*v*): soak,

Bil (*n*): taste,

Bilibili (*adj*): scrawny,

Bilo (*v*): taste,

Bin (*v*): come,

Binika (*n*): kettle,

Bino (*n*): rise,

Bino (*v*): attend,

Bino (*v*): come,

Bino atum gero ŋom (*adj*): menacing, ominous,

Bino i wic (*v*): haunt, hang around in,

Bino iwic (*adj*): haunted,

Bino iye too too (*n*): haunt,

Bino wiya atii (*v*): precede, ahead, come first,

Biritic (*n*): British,

Biskwit (*n*): biscuits,

Bit (*adj*): jagged, sharp point, sticky out, pointed, prickly, spiky,

Bit (*adj*): piercing, sharp,

Bita (*v*): coax, persuade,

Bito (*adj*): persuade, convince, tempting,

Bito (*v*): attract, cajole, coax, persuade,

Biyo (nyoŋo) (*v*): crush,

Biyo (*v*): rinse,

Biyo (*v*): squash,

Blu pere ne tye col doki bene tye doki lwar (*adj*): livid,

Bok (*n*): box

Boke pa kom ki ceŋ (*n*): sunburn,

Boko (kom) (*adj*): tan,

Boko (*v*): roast, cook,

Boko kom (*v*): bleach,

Bol (*n*): throw, toss, fling,

Bolo (ki anyot) (*v*) dump,

Bolo (*v*): toss,

Bolo (yugi) (*v*): dump,

Bolo dog (*n, leg.*): application,

Bolo gina acoya i kot (*n*): filling of document,

Bolo kwiri (*v*): vote,

Bolo piny (*n*): convulsion, fit,

Boma (*n*): trick,

Bomo (*v*): decive, fool, trick, dupe,

Bomo kom (*adj*): idealistic,

Boŋ ocoo (*adj*): unwritten,

Boŋ onoŋ (*adj*): unknown,

Boŋ onyom (*adj*): unmarried,

Boŋo (*adj*): cloth, garment, material,

Boŋo (*n*): dress, cloth,

Boŋo kor me iye (*n*): vest

Bor (*adj*): far, long, tall,

Bor (*adv*): far, distant

Bor luŋga luŋga (boŋo) (*adj*): voluminous,

Bor maleŋ (*adj*): lofty,

Boro (*adj*): cavernous,

Boro (*adj*): distant, far-away,

Boro (*n*): level, height,

Boro ne (I ca nyo ikin piny) (*adj*): far-off,

Boro ne ki yo ka piny (*adj*): wide, horizontal,

Boro ne ki yo malo (*adj*): vertical, lenth, height,

Boro piny (*n*): mile,

Bot (*prep.*): to,

Bot kom (*adj*): lazy, arid, indolent, somber, dull, boring, drab, dreary, vapid,

Boto (*v*): deter,

Botto kom dano (*adj*): dull, staid,

Boyo (*v*): wrap,

Braun (*adj*): brown,

Braun kala (*adj*): brown,

Buc (*adj*): bruised,

Buc (*n*): bruise,

Buc (*n*): Jail,

Buco (*v*): bruise,

Buk (*n*): book,

Buk (*n*): book,

Buk ma gonyo tyen lok (*n*): dictionary,

Buk me ododo (*adj*): novel,

Buko (ki raŋi) (*v*): dye,

Buko (kom,) (*v*): bleach,

Buko (*v*): colour, paint, shade, fill,

Bulo (*adj*): roasted,

Bulo (*v*): bake,

Bulo *(v)*: roast

Bulu (*adj*): blue,

Bulu (*adj*): youthful,

Bulu ma odoŋo a doŋa (*adj*): tender,

Bulu papol (*adj*): violet,

Bun (*n*): coffee,

Buny (*n*): slip,

Bunyo (*n*): smile, beam,

Bunyo (*v*): smile,

Bunyo akoda akoda (*n*): grin,

Bunyo akoda akoda (*v*): grin,

Bunyo ko (*adj*): unsmiling, deadpan,

Bunyo makwak (*n*): beam,

Bunyo makwak (*v*): beam,

Buŋa (*n*): forest,

Bur (*n*): hole, gap,

Bur (*n*): wound,

Bur ic (*n*): ulcer,

Bur ilak (*n*): cavity,

Bur magi kwinyo me golo ga magi noŋo i te ŋom (*n*): mine,

Bur me mac (*n*): plug, socket,

Bur okoro (*n*): cancer,

Bura (*adj*): menacing,

Bura (*n*): threat,

Buro (*v*): threaten,

Buru dano (*adj*): creepy, threatening,

But ceŋ yo acam ki yo wok ceŋ (*n*): North,

But ceŋ yo acwic ki yo wok ceŋ (*n*): South,

But ceŋ yo acwic ki yo wok ceŋ me Cudan (*n*): South Sudan,

Bute aŋwen ma pime weŋ maromrom (*n*): square,

Bute aŋwen ma pime weŋ maromrom ko (*n*): rectangular,

Buto (*adj*): sleeping,

Bwara (*adj*): rowdy, strident,

Bwara (*adj*): snarling, growl, roar,

Bwara (bura) (*adj*): thunderous,

Bwara (*n*): roar, snarl, thunder,

Bwara (*v*): bawl, thunder,

Bwo (calo tyen atudo) (*adj*): webbed,

Bwoc (*n*): defeat,

Bwola – ilibo (*adj*): crafty, cunning,

Bwola (*n*): trap, trick,

Bwolo (*adj*): tricky,

Bwolo (*v*): cheat, deceive, trick, swindle, defraud, dupe,

Bwom (*n*): wing,

Bwomi (*adj*): corrupt, dishonest,

Bwomi (*n*): corruption, cheating,

Bwono (ga) (*adj*): understated,

Bwot (*n*) leave, escape,

Bwoto (*adj*): deserted, abandoned, forsaken,

Bwoto (*v*): desert, drop, abandon, leave, omit, leave out, quit,

Bwoto (*v*): release,

Bwoto (*v*): retire, leave,

Bwoto (weko) (*v*): clear, free,

Bwoto jwene (*adj*): distant, aloof,

Bwoto ki dyere (*v*): suspend, hang,

Bwoto tic (*v*): retire, give up the work,

Bwoyo (*v*): overrun,

Bwoyo (*v*): subdue, subjugate, overpower,

Bwoyo kero (*v*): vanquish,

C

Caa (*n*): time, watch,

Caa abic me odi wor (*n*): eleven Oclock in the night, 11pm,

Caa abic me odiko (*n*): eleven Oclock in the morning, 11am,

Caa abicel me cwiny odi wor (*n*): twelve Oclock in the midnight, 12pm,

Caa abicel me odi ceŋ (*n*): twelve Oclock in the noon, 12noon,

Caa abiro me odi wor (*n*): one Oclock in the morning, 1am,

Caa abiro me otyeno (*n*): one Oclock in the afternoon, 1pm,

Caa aboŋwen me odi wor (*n*): three Oclock in the morining, 3am,

Caa aboŋwen me otyeno (*n*): three Oclock in the afternoon, 3pm,

Caa aboro me odi wor (*n*): two Oclock in the morning, 2am,

Caa aboro me otyeno (*n*): two Oclock in the afternoon, 2pm,

Caa acel me obwara (*n*): seven oclock in the evenining, 7pm,

Caa acel me odiko (*n*): seven oclock in the morning, 7am,

Caa adek me odi wor (*n*): nine Oclock in the night, 9pm,

Caa adek me odiko (*n*): nine colock in the morning, 9am,

Caa aŋwen me odi wor (*n*): ten Oclock in the night, 10pm,

Caa aŋwen me odiko (*n*): ten Oclock in the morning, 10am,

Caa apar me ka ru pa piny (*n*): four Oclock in the morning, 4am,

Caa apar me Otyeno (*n*): four Oclock in the afternoon, 4pm,

Caa apar wiye acel me ka ru pa piny (*n*): five Oclock in the morning, 5am,

Caa apar wiye acel me otyeno (*n*): five Oclock in the afternoon, 5pm,

Caa apar wiye ariyo me odiko (*n*): six Oclock in the morining, 6am,

Caa apar wiye ariyo me otyeno (*n*): six Oclock in the afternoon, 6pm,

Caa ariyo me obwara (*n*): eight oclock in the evening, 8pm,

Caa ariyo me odiko (*n*): eight oclock in the morning, 8am,

Caa ma (*conj*): after, once

Caa mo keken (*conj.*): whenever, everytime, what ever time, when,

Caa mukene (*adj*): occasional,

Caa mukene (*adv*): sometimes,

Caa ni (*adj*): current, present,

Cac (*adj*): sardonic, scornful, mocking, sarcastic, ironic, satirical, wry, cynical,

Caden (*adj*): evident,

Caden (*n*): record, evidence,

Caden (*n, leg.*): evidence,

Caden ma otime i kot (*n, leg.*): exhibit,

Cado (*n*): diarrhea,

Cage (*pron.*): those,

Cage ni (*adj*): those,

Cak (*n*): breast, milk,

Cak kor (*n*): breast,

Caka yu (keto wic) (*adj*): unkept,

Cakan (*n*): plate,

Caki (*v*): start, begin,

Cako (doŋo) (*v*): form, start to exist,

Cako (peko) (*v*): make, cause, produce, cause something,

Cako (*v*): begin,

Cako (*v*): create,

Cako (*v*): fire, start up,

Cako (*v*): open, begin, start,

Cako alii (*n*): stir,

Cakuc (*n*): hammer,

Cal anena (*n*): film, movie,

Cal anena wiye wiye (*n*): clip,

Cal me iwic (*adj*): fancy,

Cal me poyo wic (*adj*): monument,

Calo (*adj*): like,

Calo (*adj*): likely, probable,

Calo (*conj.*): as, like,

Calo (*prep.*): as, like, similar to,

Calo (*prep.*): near, like,

Calo …ko (*prep.*): unlike,

Calo i (*prep.*): as,

Calo lamaika (*adj*): angelic, relating to angels,

Calo latin (*adj*): babyish, childish, infantile, immature,

Calo odii (*adj*): buttery,

Cam (*n*): produce, farm or garden products,

Camo (*v*): eat, consume, have a meal,

Campu (*n*): shampoo,

Can (*adj*): poor,

Can (*n*): need, poverty, want, poor,

Canduk (*n*): box,

Cani (*adj*): desire, yearn for,

Cani (*adj*): envy,

Cani (*adj*): that,

Cani (*pron.*): that,

Cano (*v*): arrange, position, assemble,

Cany (*n*): throw, toss,

Canyo (*v*): throw,

Caŋ (*n*): cure, treatment,

Caŋo (*v*): cure, heal, cure,

Car (mac) (*adj*): bright, brilliant

Caricari (*adj*): clumsy

Caro (*adj*): irresponsible, careless, reckless, negligent, shoddy,

Caro (*adj*): remote, rural,

Caro (*adj*): sparkling, luminous, radiant, dazzling, gleaming, shining, bright,

Caro (leb) (*adj*): coarse (language),

Caro (waŋ) (*adj*): reflecting,

Caro piny maleŋ (*adv*): brightly, luminous, radiantly,

Cat (*n*): trade, commerce,

Cat manyen (*n*): venture,

Catan (*n*): Satan,

Cati (*n*): shirt,

Cato (*v*): sell, deals, trade, fetch, be sold,

Cato cat (*v*): trade,

Cattan (*n*): Saturn,

Cayo (*v*): criticize, jeer, overlook, sneer,

Cayo cwiny (*v*): exempt,

Cayo kom (*n*): risk, venture,

Cayo kom (wot ka marac) (*v*): venture,

Cek (*v*): heat,

Cek makwar (go yo waŋ ki lworo) (*adj*): blushing,

Cel (*n*): fence,

Celo (muduku) (*v*): drill, fire, shoot,

Celo (*v*): fry,

Celo teretere (*v*): barrage,

Cen (*adv*): down, behind,

Cen (*n*): curse,

Cen marac (*n*): evil spirit, devil,

Cene (*n*): money,

Cene acula (*n*): bill,

Cene adit adit (*n*): change,

Cene ma gi coyo i di waraga (*n*): check,

Cene ma myero otii kede teretere (*adj*): outgoing,

Ceno (*v*): curse,

Ceŋ (*n*): sun,

Ceŋ Abic (*n*): Friday,

Ceŋ Abicel (*n*): Saturday,

Ceŋ Adek (*n*): Wednesday,

Ceŋ Aŋwen (*n*): Thursday,

Ceŋ Ariyo (*n*): Tuesday,

Ceŋ Baraja (*n*): Monday,

Ceŋ Cabit (*n*): Sunday,

Ceŋeŋe (*n*): grate,

Cer (*n*): highlight,

Cer (*v*): rise, wake up,

Cere (*adj*): daring

Cere (me time gi moni) (*v*): venture,

Cere (*v*): challenge, dare,

Cere cere (bit) (*adj*): jagged,

Ceregel (*n*): earthworm,

Cero (lok): (*v*): argue,

Cero (pyem) (*adj*): defensive,

Cero (tur nyim, kom) (*v*): brand,

Cero (*v*): highlight,

Cero (*v*): maintain, argue,

Cero (*v*): row,

Cero (*v*): trace,

Cero (yeya) (*v*): paddle,

Cero lok (*adj*): querulous, argumentative,

Cero lok (*n*): debate, row, disagreement,

Cero lok (*n, leg*): dissent,

Cero lok (*n, leg.*): issues,

Cero lok (*v*): debate,

Cero piny kilokilo (boŋo) (*adj*): fray,

Cero rek (*v*): bar,

Cet (*n*): waste, excrement,

Ci (*adv*): accordingly, therefore,

Ci (*adv*): accordingly, therefore,

Ci doŋ (*adv*): hence,

Cidi (*n*): CD,

Cido (*v*): shade, darken,

Cido cwiny (*v*): bore,

Cido waŋ (*v*): cross, thwart,

Cik (me niye) (*n*): guarantee, assuarance, promise, pledge,

Cik (*n*): dictate, priniciple,

Cik (*n*): rule, law, discipline, regulation, order, instruction,

Cik (*n, leg.*): constitution,

Cik (*n, leg.*): law, rules,

Cik akwaya (*n, leg.*): act, bill,

Cik akwaya pa dul me keto cik (*n, leg.*): statutes,

Cik ducu (*n, leg.*): common law,

Cik ma kwako dano (*n, leg.*): civil law,

Cik ma oketo piny (*n, leg*): regulation,

Cik magi moko (ma tye atir doki ca mukene petye atir ento tye kakare) (*adj*): ethical,

Cik me bal (ma mako twero pa dano ki lotic weŋ) (*n, leg.*): criminal law,

Cik me nam (*n, leg.*): admiralty,

Cik me tekwaro (*n, leg.*): customary law,

Cik me tela (*n, leg.*): administrative law,

Cik me yer (cimo ŋa ma myero gilwoŋ i kot) (*n, leg.*): rules of standing,

Cik mo keken ma oyee iye (*n, leg.*): statutory rule,

Cik oyee (*adj*): legal,

Cikke (*n*): meeting, appointment,

Ciko (*v*): guarantee, assure, ensure, promise, pledge, warrant, certify, enjoin, command,

Ciko waŋ (*adj*): glaring,

Ciko waŋ (*v*): stare,

Cikweya (*n*): Square

Cil cwiny (*adj*): austere, robust, severe, strict, stern, grave, sober, ascetic, serious, rigorous,

Cilo (*adj*): dirty, dirt, drab, dusty, filthy, grubby,

Cilo (*n*): stain,

Cilo (pii): murky,

Cilo muton (*n*): blot,

Cim (*n*): phone, telephone, call, mobile,

Cim (*n*): point, aim,

Cime (*adj*): impressive,

Cime ko (*adj*): awkward,

Cimo (*v*): name, nominate, point, postulate, aim,

Cimo lok iwic (*v*): warn,

Cin (*n*): colon, appendix, stomach,

Cin ic (*n*): stomach, intestine, womb, uterus,

Ciŋ (*n*): hand,

Ciŋe tek (*adj*): miserly,

Ciŋe yot (*adj*): deft,

Cipanic (*adj*): Spanish,

Cipinja (*n*): slipper,

Cire ko (*adj*): unbearable,

Ciro (*adj*): enduring, abiding,

Ciro (*v*): bear, endure,

Ciro kec (*adj*): fast

Citi (*v*), move, go,

Cito (*v*): attend,

Cito (*v*): go, head, travel,

Cito ka ywe (*v*): retire, go to bed,

Cob (*n*): stab,

Cobo (*adj*): successful,

Cobo (*n*): poke, prod,

Cobo (*v*): perform, accomplish,

Cobo (*v*): stab, knife,

Cobo i (*v*): control, manage,

Cobo miti (*v*): contend,

Coc (*n*) type, key up,

Coc magi tamo iye doki tyeŋ (*adj*): poetic,

Coc me diri (*n*): print, font,

Coda (*n*): soda,

Coge ki rek (*n*): train, procession,

Cogo (*adj*): skeletal,

Cogo (*n*): bone,

Cok (*adj*): close, near,

Cok (*adv*): about, almost,

Cok (*adv*): soon,

Cok (*prep.*): near, close to,

Cok cok (*adj*): frequently, often, regularly, normally, commonly, recurrently, habitually, repeatedly,

Cok cok (*adv*): habitually, repeatedly,

Cok cok (*adv*): often,

Cok cok ni (*adj*): recent,

Cok cok ni (*adv*): recently,

Cok cwiny (*n*): emotion,

Cok cwiny (ŋet pa cwiny) (*adj*): testy,

Cok kede (*adv*): closely,

Cok kedi (*adj*): neighbour, next,

Cok ki (*adv*): nearby,

Cok ki (*prep.*): around, close to,

Cok ne (*adv*): nearly,

Cok romo (*prep.*): around, about,

Coko (*v*): clear, tidy, collect, gather, pack,

Coko kacel (*n*): pack,

Coko muŋ (ki bot lomone nyo jo ma wu pyemo ked gi) (*adj*): intelligent,

Col (*adj*): dark, black,

Col acola (*adj*): murky,

Col cwiny (a*dj*): cruel, vicious,

Col piny (*adj*): dark,

Col ripiripi (*adj*): gray,

Cola acola (waŋ): gloomy,

Comalia (*n*): Somalia,

Con (*adj*): early,

Con (*adj*): old,

Con (*adv*): early,

Con (oyot) (*adv*): quicker,

Con ki con (*adv*): previously,

Con ki con (*prep.*) before, previous to,

Coŋ (*n*): knee,

Coo (*n*): porcupine,

Coo (*v*): wake,

Cora acora (*adj*): clumsy,

Core (ki lok) (*v*): blurt,

Core (kot) (*v*): pelt,

Core (*v*): jolt,

Core doki pwa (kot) (*adj*): teeming,

Coro (*adj*): repulsive,

Coto (*adj*): filthy, muddy,

Coto (*n*): mud,

Coyabin (*n*): soya bean,

Coyo (*adj*): spotted,

Coyo (kodi) (*v*): sow,

Coyo (taipiŋ) (*v*): type,

Coyo (*v*): awake,

Coyo (*v*): brand,

Coyo (*v*): print, publish, utter,

Coyo (*v*): write,

Coyo cik (me Kompita,) (*v*): program,

Coyo coc i kom lok moni (*n*): discourse,

Coyo di waraga (*v*): file,

Coyo kom (*n*): rash,

Coyo piny (*v*): note,

Coyo piny (*v*): record,

Cudan (*n*): Sudan,

Cuk (*n*): market,

Cuka (*n*): bed sheet,

Cukari (*n*): sugar,

Cuko cwiny (*v*): prompt, encourage, give confidence,

Cul (*n*): cost, outlay, expense,

Cul (*n*): pay, wage,

Cul (*n*): rate, charge,

Cul (*n, leg.*): damages,

Cul pa gamente bot ŋat ma pe onoŋo tic (*n*): dole,

Cul pa latic me cik ma ocuŋo pi dul moni (*n, leg*): professional costs,

Culo (*adj*): back, sponsor, support, assist, finance (*lit.*) paying

Culo (*v*): pay, settle,

Culo cul pa gamente bot ŋat ma pe onoŋo tic (*v*): dole,

Culo kwor (*adj*): vengeful, revengeful,

Cumari (*n*): nail,

Cun (yet) (*n*): penis,

Cuno (*v*): engage,

Cuŋ (*n*): stand,

Cuŋ (*n*): stop,

Cuŋ (*v*): rise, stand up,

Cuŋ koŋ (*n*): stay, halt,

Cuŋo (*adj*): responsible,

Cuŋo (*n*): ban, prohibition,

Cuŋo (*v*): cut, stop,

Cuŋo (*v*): assert,

Cuŋo (*v*): bar, ban,

Cuŋo (*v*): brake, end, stop,

Cuŋo (*v*): land, settle,

Cuŋo (*v*): stand,

Cuŋo cam (*n*): diet,

Cuŋo i lok (*adj*): responsible,

Cuŋo iye (*v*): maintain,

Cuŋo iye (*v*): operate, manage, uphold,

Cuŋo iye ko (*adj*): irresponsible, careless, negligent,

Cuŋo ko (*adj*): nonstop,

Cuŋo manok (*v*): pause,

Cuŋo matek (*adj*): robust,

Cuŋo matek ko (*adj*): floppy,

Cuŋo mutukari (*v*): park,

Cuŋo pi (*v*): present, stand for, portray, represent,

Cuŋo pi en (*v*): recommend, advocate,

Cuŋo pi kare manok (*n*): stay, halt,

Cuŋo pi kare manok (*v*): hang, suspend, postpone,

Cuŋo rok rok (*v*): challenge, confront,

Cuŋo waŋ ki waŋ (*v*): face, confront,

Cuŋo wic (*adj*): puzzle, bewilder, perplex, baffle, mystify,

Cuŋo wic (*v*): confused,

Cupa (*n*): bottle,

Cupuria (*n*): saucepan,

Cur (*n*): grunt, moan, groan,

Cur (pa latin) (*adj*): cooing,

Cur (*v*): grunt, moan,

Curu me remo (*n*): blood pressure,

Curuwal (*n*): pair of short,

Custa (*n*): zip,

Cut (*n*): suit,

Cutcut (*adv*): suddenly,

Cwak (*adj*): partial, biased, prejudiced,

Cwak (gamo lok) (*n. leg*): defence,

Cwak (*n*): jaw, molar,

Cwako (*adj*): second, support, agree with, back up, go along with, be with,

Cwako (*v*): applaud, approve, assert, support,

Cwal (*n*): sack,

Cwal (*v*): submit,

Cwalo (dwan) (*v*): emit,

Cwalo (*v*): drive, push,

Cwalo (*v*): recommend, commend,

Cwalo (*v*): send, mail, post,

Cwalo dwan (*v*): sound,

Cwalo dwan (*v*): utter,

Cwalo kwena (radio, cal, telebicon) (*n*): broadcast,

Cwalo kwena ki radiyo nyo Telebicion (*v*): beam,

Cwe (*adj*): fat

Cwec (*n*): build, shape,

Cwer (*adj*): profuse, runny,

Cwer (*v*): rain,

Cwer cwiny (*adj*): sorrowful, sad, mournful, grief-stricken, distressed, unhappy, upset, depressed,

Cwer cwiny (*adv*): sadly,

Cwer cwiny (*n*): shock, upset, worry, concern,

Cwer kom (*adj*): lazy,

Cwer pa remo (*n*): bleed,

Cwero cwiny (*v*): upset, worry,

Cwero cwiny dano makwak (*adj*): tragic,

Cwero kom dano acwera (*adj*): tedious,

Cwero remo (*v*): bleed,

Cweyo (*v*): build, create,

Cwic (*n*): hiss, jeer, jeering, booing,

Cwiny (*adj*): spiritual, inward,

Cwiny (*n*): spirit,

Cwiny dano pe iye (*adj*): uninteresting,

Cwiny iye (*adj*): attentive, eager,

Cwiny iye (*n*): interest, desire,

Cwiny maleŋ (*n*): Holy Spirit,

Cwiny mito (*adj*): willing,

Cwiny mito ko (*adv*): unwillingly,

Cwiny pe iye (*adj*): tepid, lukewarm, unenthuasiastic,

Cwiny pe iye (*adj*): drab, dull,

Cwinye cil (*adj*): brave, courageous,

Cwinye cok (*adj*): emotional,

Cwinye cok ko (*adv*): unemotionally,

Cwinye cok rye (*adj*): impassioned, passion,

Cwinye kore (*adj*): anxious, nervous, worried, concerned, uneasy, apprehensive, restless, fretful,

Cwinye kuta kuta (*adj*): ecstatic, infatuated, obsessed,

Cwinye kwero (*adj*): repulsive,

Cwinye leŋ (*adj*): generous, kind, liberal, bighearted, openhanded, munificient, giving, charitable, altruistic,

Cwinye obuto iye doki kodo (*adj*): wary,

Cwinye obutu iye (*adj*): uptight, nervous, anxiety,

Cwinye pe cok (*adj*): stable, unemotional,

Cwinye pe iye (*adj*): uninterested, half-hearted,

Cwinye pe ka nyero ne (*adj*): faint,

Cwinye pe kaloke ne (*adj*): faint,

Cwinye tek (*adj*): brave, courageous, fearless

Cwinye tye (*adj*): eager, keen, enthusiastic, willing, ready,

Cwinye weŋ (*adj*): earnest, very serious,

Cwinye yom (*adj*): happy,

Cwinye yom (*adv*): glady,

Cwinyo (mac) (*v*): spark,

Cwinyo (pii) (*v*): blot,

Cwinyo pii (*v*): drain,

Cwire (*n*): kissing,

Cwire (*v*): hiss, jeer,

Cwiyo (*v*): snicker,

Cwiyo ne (dwan) (*adj*): hissing,

D

Daa (*n*): argument, quarrel, row, disagreement,

Daa (*v*): quarrel, argue,

Dak cwiny (*adj*): hateful, abhorrent, distasteful, disgusting, detestable,

Dako (*adj*): female,

Dako (*n*): woman,

Dako ma lacat (*n*): business woman,

Dako pere otoo oko (*n*): window (male),

Daktar (*n*): doctor,

Daktar me lak (*n*): dentist,

Dano (*n*): people,

Dano adana (*adj*): mortal, human being,

Dano ma ŋere (*n*): star, famous, celebrity,

Dano nyo dul pa dano dek ma donyo iye (*adj*): triangular,

Danyo (*n*): rainbow,

Daŋe (*n*): shout

Daŋe (*n*): sway, dangle,

Daŋe (*v*): bawl, shout,

Daŋe (*v*): exclaim,

Daŋe (*v*): sway, swing,

Daŋo cwiny (*adj*): shocked,

Dar (ceŋ, mac) (*adj*): dazzling, glittery, glittering,

Dar (ceŋ, mac) (*n*): beam,

Dar (*n*): beam, ray,

Dar ceŋ (*n*): sun shine,

Datoo (*n*): widow (female),

Dayo (*n*): grand mother,

Dayo madit (*n*): great grand mother,

Dec (*v*): choke,

Dek (*n*): sauce, food,

Del (*n*): hide, pelt, skin,

Del kom mutwo mawanye awanya (*adj*): scaly,

Den (*n*): loan,

Deno (*v*): borrow,

Deno (*v*): owe,

Der (*v*): tire,

Dere (*n*): wrestle,

Dere (*v*): wrestle,

Derebe (*n*): driver,

Dero (*adj*): tire, jaded, world –weary, tired, worn –out, fed-up, bored,

Dero (*n*): barn,

Det (*adj*): insidious,

Det (*n*): infection,

Deyo (*adj*): glorious, majestic,

Deyo (*n*): glory, grace, elegance,

Deyo (orwate ki kabaka ki mukene) ((*adj*): regal,

Deyo (*v*): decorate,

Deyo (*v*): hang, lynch,

Di tyelo (*n*): foot,

Dic (*n*): force, influence, pressure,

Dic (*n*): stress,

Didit (*adj*): substantial, sizeable, considerate, extensive,

Dido (*n*): challenge,

Dido (*v*): highlight, emphasize,

Dido lok (*adj*): curious, inquisitive, inquiring,

Dii (*adj*): attached, (*lit*) press,

Dii cwinyi (*adj*): cool, calm down,

Diiŋ (*adj*): narrow, tight,

Dikdik ko (tic) (*adv*): casual,

Diki (*adv*): tomorrow,

Dimadima (*adj*): dull,

Diŋ (*adj*): tight,

Diŋ it (*n*): deaf,

Diŋo (yat) (*adj*): sedate,

Diŋo waŋ (*n*): gesture,

Diŋo waŋ (*v*): wink,

Diradira (*adj*): deficient, failing or short coming

Dire (*adj*): advanced,

Dire (*n*): move, shift, step,

Dire (*v*): move, reposition,

Dire ko (*adj*): unwielded,

Diri (*adj*): diligent, subtle,

Diri (*adj*): innovative,

Diri ki rwom (*adj*): solemn,

Diri mo pe iye (*adj*): informal,

Diro (*v*): get, move, shift,

Diro piny (*v*): lower,

Dit (*adj*): big, substantial, large, considerate, huge, mammoths, colossal, gigantic, great,

Dit (ga nyo dano) (*adj*) jumbo,

Dit (ki guro) (*adj*): grand, large,

Dit cwiny (*adj*): ambitious, avaricious, pushy,

Dit kato weŋ (*adj*): tremendous,

Dit loyo weŋ (*adj*): fabulous, fantastic, huge, great, ernomous, tremendous, very big, very large, prodigious, gigantic, terrific, colossal, immense,

Dit loyo weŋ (*adv*): tremendously,

Dit makato (*adj*): whopping,

Dit makwak (*adj*): colossal, huge, massive, immense, oversize, gigantic, enormous, gargantuan, large, vast, monumental,

Dit te (*adv*): mainly,

Dit twatwal (*adj*): huge, immense,

Dite (*n*): highlight,

Dite (*n*): measure,

Dite (*n*): size,

Diyo (*adj*) pressing, stress, bleak, depressing, burdensome, oppressive, failing, forceful, gloomy, grim,

Diyo (*n*): pinch,

Diyo (*v*): dial, press, push,

Diyo (*v*): force, drive,

Diyo ciŋ (*v*): sign,

Diyo ciŋ (*v*): stamp, imprint,

Diyo cwiny (*adj*): patient, mortified,

Diyo dano (*adj*): pushy, aggressive, forceful, damaging, depressing, down beat, negative,

Diyo dwane (*adj*): squeaky,

Diyo dwane koŋ manok (*adj*): muted,

Doge (*n*): cover,

Doge bit (akoda nyo nyo Waco lok): pungent,

Doge cere cere (*adj*): jagged,

Doge ma opoto (*n*): flap,

Doge ma otude (*n*): knot,

Doge pe (*adj*): deadpan, expressionless, straight –faced, pokerfaced,

Dok (*n*): fall, drop, descent,

Dok (*n*): mouth,

Dok (*v*): fall, drop,

Dok aŋec (*n*): reverse,

Dok cen (*v*): back,

Dok piny (*n*): drop, reduction, fall, cut,

Doki a ka (*adv*): deliberately, intentionally,

Doki acac (*adj*): several, mumerous, quite a lot,

Doki acac (*adv*): abundantly, plenty off

Doki aka (*adv*): willfully,

Doki bulu (*adv*): youthfully,

Doki gero (*adv*): wildly,

Doki gi me tim (*adv*): wildly,

Doki lanede (*adv*): elegantly,

Doki liwot (*adj*): friendly,

Doki too (*adv*): again, once more,

Doki won twero (*adv*): responsibly,

Doko tyen ariyo (*v*) double,

Dol (kom) (*n*): twists,

Dol (*n*): coil, curl,

Dol (*n*): fold,

Dole (*v*): balk, shy away,

Dolo (*v*): bend, curve, twist, coil, curl, fold,

Donyo (lweny (*v*): storm,

Donyo (*v*): enter, go into, go through,

Donyo i lok (*v*): pry, interfere, poke, concern, relate to, snoop,

Doŋ (*n*): pat,

Doŋ (*v*): remain, stay,

Doŋe (*n*): balance,

Doŋo (*adj*): great,

Doŋo (*adj*): growing, grown,

Doŋo (*n*): rise, growth,

Doŋo (*v*): develop, grow, form,

Doŋo (*v*): pat,

Doŋo (*v*): slap, hit, knock, bash,

Doŋo ciŋ (*n*): clap,

Doŋo ciŋ (*v*): applaud, clap,

Doŋo gumi (*n*): ring, boxing,

Doŋo kor (*n*): dare,

Doŋo oduru (*v*): shout, ululate, howl, scream, shriek, wail, cry, yell,

Doŋo oduru ki dwan maliu (*v*): shriek,

Doo (*n*): weed,

Dor (*n*): draw, sketch,

Dore (*n*): march, demonstration,

Dore (*v*): march,

Doro (*v*): draw, sketch,

Doro wic (*adj*): flustered,

Doro wiye wiye (*v*): sketch,

Doto (*v*): report, give an account,

Ducu (*adj*): all, general, universal, unanimous, universal, all-purposes, wide-ranging, broad, common, broad-spectrum,

Dukan (*n*): shop,

Dul (ma laro lok i kot) (*n, leg.*): parties,

Dul (*n*): cell, group,

Dul (*n*): order, association, combines,

Dul (*n*): set, collection,

Dul (pa lotim aranyi) (*n*): ring, group,

Dul me keto cik (*n, leg.*): statues,

Dul me lok ma ocuŋo pire kene *(n)*: sentence,

Dul pa dano (*n*): crush, crowd, throng,

Dule (*adj*): total,

Duny (*v*): evaporate,

Duny (*v*): fume,

Dunyo (*v*): brush, sweep,

Dunyo (*v*): emit,

Dunyo (*v*): polish,

Dunyo (*v*): rub,

Dunyo (*v*): wipe,

Dunyo luru (*v*): dust,

Dwalo (*v*): twist,

Dwan (*n*): tune, sound, voice, note,

Dwan (*n*): throat,

Dwan mamit (*adj*): melodic,

Dwane leŋ (*adj*): Melodic

Dwane malo (*adj*): deafening, noisy, vociferous, loud,

Dwane rwate (*n*): rhyme,

Dwanye (*adj*): serpentine, winding, meandering, twisting, bending,

Dwanye (pa kulu) (*v*): wander, meander,

Dwanyo (*adj*): squiggly,

Dwanyo coc (*n*): scribble,

Dwanyo coc (*v*): scribble,

Dwar (*n*) search, hunt, hunting,

Dwaro (*v*): hunt,

Dwayo (*v*): drive, give somebody a ride, steer,

Dwayo (*v*): twist,

Dwayo mutukari (*n*): ride,

Dwayo wi dano ki kom lok (*adj*): extraneous, irrelevant, unrelated, inappropriate,

Dwayo wi dano ki kom lok (*adj*): inappropriate,

Dwe (*n*): moon,

Dwe me Abic (*n*): May,

Dwe me Abicel (*n*): June,

Dwe me Abiro (*n*): July,

Dwe me Aboŋwen (*n*): Septemeber,

Dwe me Aboro (*n*): August,

Dwe me Acel (*n*): January,

Dwe me Adek (*n*): March,

Dwe me Aŋwen (*n*): April,

Dwe me Apar (*n*): October,

Dwe me Apar wiye Acel (*n*): November,

Dwe me Apar wiye Ariyo (*n*): December,

Dwe me Ariyo (*n*): February,

Dwero lok (*v*): disclose, reveal,

Dwir (*adj*): fast,

Dwiro (*adj*): speedy,

Dwiro (*n*): rate, speed,

Dwogi (*v*): return, comeback,

Dwogo (*adj*): back, (*lit*) coming back,

Dwogo (*v*): return,

Dwogo i waŋ (*adj*): reflecting,

Dwogo i waŋ (*v*): reflect,

Dwogo i wic (*v*): haunt, appear,

Dwogo lawaŋe dyaŋ (*v*): counter, counteract,

Dwogo yo aŋec (*v*): reverse, overturn,

Dwoko (*v*): reduce,

Dwoko kom piny (*adj*): simplistic,

Dwoko piny (*v*): lower,

Dwoko waŋe (*v*): replace, put back,

Dwoko wel mucara piny (*v*): dock,

Dwonŋe (*pron.*): most,

Dwoŋ (*adj*): many, a lot of, numerous

Dwoŋ atta (*adj*): bountiful, plentiful, numerous,

Dwoŋ atta (*adv*): abundantly, plenty off, existing in a large quantities,

Dwoŋ ko (*adj*): few, small number, the minority

Dyak (*adj*): wet, damp, soaked, soaking, soggy, sopping, dripping, moist, watery,

Dyak ki moo (*v*): oil, lubricate,

Dyak makwak (*v*): drenched,

Dyaŋ (*n*): cattle,

Dyaŋ madako (*n*): cow,

Dyeny (*n*): wave,

Dyenyo (i kin lwak,) (*v*): plow, cut through something,

E

Ee eni (*adv*): recently,

Ejipt (*n*): Egypt,

Ekcrei (macin) (*n*): x-ray,

El (*n*): lift,

Ele (*n*): rise,

Elip (*n*): thousand,

Elo (*v*): raise, lift,

Elo cwiny (*v*): inspire, motivate,

Em (*n*): thigh,

En (*pron.*): she, he, him, her, it,

En ben ye (on board) (*adv*): aboard

En bene ye (*adj*): aboard, onboard, involved

En kene (*adv*): solely,

En ki kome (*pron.*): himself, herself, itself,

Eni (*adj*): this,

Enoni (*adj*): these,

Ento (*adv*) unfortunately, however, nevertheless,

Ento (*conj.*): yet, but, however, neverthelsess,

Ento (*prep.*): but,

Etiopia (*n*): Ethiopia,

G

Ga (*adj*): material,

Ga (*n*): stuff, material, possessions, object, thing,

Ga ma pire tek (*n*): supply,

Ga ma tye liri liri (*n*): strip,

Ga me cak (*n*): dairy products,

Ga mo keken ma tye i kin piny (*n*): matter,

Ga mogo iwic (*n*): influence, effect,

Ga weŋ (*pron.*): everything,

Gacia (*n*): cassia,

Gak (*v*): preserve, maintain,

Galam (*n*): pen,

Gale (*n*): delay, lateness,

Gale (*v*): delay,

Galo wic (ki a koda) (*v*): amuse,

Galo wic (*v*): entertain, amuse,

Gamente (*n*): government,

Gamo (lok) (*v*): break, end silence,

Gamo (*v*): answer, receive, acknowledge, reply,

Gamo (*v*): greet, reply something,

Gamo dwan (*n*): echo,

Gamo dwan (*v*): echo,

Gamo lok (cwak i kot) (*n, leg.*): reply,

Gamo lok ko (*adj*): unresponsive,

Gamo mac (*n*): spark,

Gamo waŋ (*adj*): rewarding,

Gamo waŋ (*v*): satisfy,

Gaŋ (*n*): place, home,

Gaŋ kal madit (*adj*): urban,

Gaŋ Kwan (*n*): college,

Gaŋ Kwan ma malo (*n*): University,

Gaŋ Kwan me ariyo (*n*): secondary school,

Gaŋ Kwan pa Ludoŋo (*n*): adult education,

Gaŋi madoŋo (*adj*): urban,

Gar (*n*): train,

Gayo ki te waŋ (*v*): ogle,

Gela (*adj*): adolescent,

Gemo (*adj*): fatal, deadly, lethal, incurable, terminal,

Gen (*adj*): hopeful, assured, confident, faithful,

Gen (*adv*): assuredly, confident,

Gen (*n*): hope, trust,

Gen pe (*adj*): hopeless, bleak,

Gene (*adj*): reliable, rosy, optimistic, bright, promising, hopeful, trustworthy, honest, truthful, reliable, unfailing,

Gene ko (*adj*): crooked, (*lit.*) dishonest, dangerous, dodgy, shady, dishonest,

Gene ko (*adj*): treacherous, unfaithful,

Gene wa (*adj*): dependable,

Geno (*adj*) (wat, kore, te gicaa,) (*adj*): assured,

Geno (*adj*): trusting,

Geno (*adv*) (wat, kore, te gicaa,) (*adv*): assuredly,

Geno (*v*): hope, rely, trust, pray,

Geno kom (*adj*): self –assured,

Geŋ (*n*): ban, prohibition, stop,

Geŋo (*n*): drag, hindrance,

Geŋo (*v*): ban, prevent, forbid, bar, stop, hinder, restrain, suppress, hold back,

Ger (*adj*): aggressive, violent, hostile, forceful, antagonistic, abrasive, rude, gruff, cruel, fierce, filthy, intense, heavy, ruthless,

Gero (*adj*): violent, vicious, deafening, riotous, wild, untamed,

Gero (pa le tim) *(adj)*: vicious,

Gero (*v*): build,

Geyo (*v*): wipe,

Gi caa (*n*): sack,

Gi kome (*n*): state, nervous, upset, or excited condition,

Gi ma gi puyo iwi gina acama (calo mugati) (*n*): paste, food spread,

Gi ma ŋic (*n*): soft drink,

Gi ma teŋe rom ko (*adj*): oblong,

Gi me cano waraga (*n*): file, folder,

Gi me coc (*n*): computer,

Gi me dino coc (i kom waraga,) (*n*): stamp,

Gi me diŋo ga (*n*): anaesthetic,

Gi me geŋo nywal (*n*): conceptrative pill,

Gi me guro waraga (*n*): file, folder,

Gi me gwoko kom (*n*): cover, shelter,

Gi me i di yamo (*n*): online,

Gi me jiŋo ga (*n*): freezer,

Gi me kweyo ga ma ŋic (*n*): fridge,

Gi me mako dwan (*n*): record,

Gi me neno cal (*n*): television,

Gi me ŋono ga (calo waraga,) (*n*): clip,

Gi me tim (*adj*): wild, undomesticated,

Gi me umo waŋ ot *(n)*: blind

Gi me wel (*adj*): luxurious,

Gi me wel mamalo (*adj*): luxurious, posh,

Gi me wer (*n*): record, disc,

Gi me yubo i dek (*adj*): spicy,

Gi mi gobo ga (*n*): scrape,

Gi mi iwic (tam) (*adj*): fancy,

Gi mi lobo (*adv*): material,

Gi mo tye i wiye (*adv*): crazy, illogically, witlessly, frantically, eccentrically,

Gi mo tye iwiye (*n*): mad, crazy,

Gi mu dok yo ikom (*adj*): physical,

Gi piyo oyot (*adj*): gullible, impressionable, easily influenced,

Gi tye ki arem (*v*): ache, pain, hurt,

Gi yubo ki ciŋ (*adj*): unnatural, artificial,

Gibegu me te layot (*n*): handbag,

Gicaa (*n*): sack,

Gicai (*n*): tea,

Gido (*v*): tickle,

Gigure (*adj*): Composed, collected, self- possessed,

Gijoge (*adj*): Composed, collected, self- possessed,

Gik ko (*adj*): infinite,

Gik ko (*adv*): endlessly,

Giko (lok marac) (*v*): break, end bad situation,

Giko (*v*): contain, control,

Giko (*v*): end,

Gikome (*adj*): classic,

Gilac (*adj*): glass,

Gilac (*n*): glass,

Gilaŋo (*n*): boil,

Gimi tiŋo dano ikin ot (*n*): lift,

Gimi wic (*adj*): fantastic, ecentric, imaginary, fanciful,

Gimi wot (*n*): transport,

Gin (*pron.*): they, them,

Gin a apwonya (*n*): program, curriculum,

Gin acoya (*n*): document, file, note, record, paper work,

Gin amata ma ŋic (*n*): soft drink, juice,

Gin apwonya (*n*): subject,

Gin ki kom gi (*pron.*): themselves,

Gin mo (*pron.*): something,

Gin mo keken (*pron.*): anything,

Gin weŋ (*pron*): both,

Gina acoya ma lwoŋo ŋat ma lomitoni kapido iye ikot (*n, leg.*): summons,

Gina acoya magi kwoŋo iye (*n*): affidavit,

Gina acoyo ma lwoŋo ŋat mo kapido i kot (*n, leg*): subpoena,

Gina amata ma ŋic (*n*): soft drink,

Gina apita (yat, dek) (*n*): plant,

Gina apwonya (*n*): program, curriculum,

Gina aruka (*n*): cloth,

Gina ura (*n*): wonder,

Gina ura madit (*adj*): remarkable, extraordinary, amazing, outstanding, noteworthy, siginificant, incredible, astonishing,

Giŋi (*adj*): austere, severe, strict, stern, grave, serious, rigorous, plain, fussy,

Giŋi: (*adj*) nagging,

Giteyi (*n*): dress,

Gitungulu (*n*): onion,

Gitwero (*n*): permit, license,

Goba (*adj*): untrue,

Goba (*n*): lying, dishonesty,

Gobo (*v*): scrape,

Goc (*n*): beat, blow, punch, hitting, beating,

Goco (*n*): playing (instrument e.g harps)

Gog (*n*): shoulder,

Goli (*n*): hook,

Golo (*v*): dig, excavate,

Golo (*v*): hook,

Gomo (*v*): curve,

Gony (*n*): camping,

Gonyo (*v*): deliver,

Gonyo (*v*): unfasten, untie,

Gonyo te coc (*v*): translate,

Gonyo te lok (*v*): interpret,

Goŋo lok (*v*): equivocate,

Gore (*adj*): fighting,

Gore (*n*): fighting, beating,

Goro (*adj*): weak, breakable, delicate, fragile, delicate, brittle, frail, precious, (*lit.*) weak, flaw, weakness, flimsy, frail, in poor health, feeble,

Goro (*n*): weak,

Goro lok ikom (*adj*): suspicious, suspect,

Got (*n*): mountain,

Goyo (*adj*): assault,

Goyo (bwoyo) (*v*): trounce,

Goyo (dunyo) (*v*): burnish, polish,

Goyo (gita) (*v*): strum,

Goyo (olaŋ, telepon) (*v*): ring,

Goyo (*v*): beat, hit, punch, bang,

Goyo (*v*): tap,

Goyo (*v*): whip,

Goyo boŋo (*v*): iron,

Goyo bwom (*v*): flap,

Goyo cim (*v*): phone, riniging telephone,

Goyo gog (*n*): shrug,

Goyo gumi (*n*): boxing,

Goyo ki muzinga (*v*): bomb,

Goyo ki oddo me kriket (*v*): bat,

Goyo laa (*n*): blessing,

Goyo tam (*v*): imagine,

Goyo tam (*v*): sneeze,

Goyo teretere (*v*): pelt,

Goyo waŋ (*v*): blink,

Goyo waŋ iye (*v*): spot,

Goyo wel (*v*): calculate, quote, give an estimate,

Gubo (*v*): sip,

Gude ko (*adj*): dangerous, unsafe,

Gudo (*n*): touch,

Gudo (*v*): handle, touch,

Gudu (*n*): road,

Gulo (*n*): sprout, shoot,

Gulo (*v*): bend, curve,

Gulo (*v*): shoot,

Gum (*adj*): blessing, grace,

Gum (*n*): blessing,

Gum kom (*adj*): lucky, fortunate, chance, providential, opportune, auspicious,

Gum kom ko (*adj*): unfortunate,

Gunya (*n*): monkey, gorilla, ape,

Guŋo (*adj*): bowed,

Guŋo (*v*): bow, kneel,

Guova (*n*): guava,

Gure (*v*): besiege,

Gure (*v*): form,

Gure (*v*): gather,

Gure (*v*): settle, land,

Guro (*v*): drive, hammer, nail, peg,

Guro kacel (*n*): pack,

Guro lwak (*v*): crowd,

Guru muŋ (ki bot lomone nyo jo ma wu pyemo ked gi) (*adj*): intelligent,

Guti (*adj*): structural,

Guti (*n*): beam, girder, frame, structure, pole,

Gutiya (*n*): sack,

Guyo (*n*): bark,

Guyo (*v*): bark,

Gwado (*v*): scratch,

Gwana (*n*): cassava,

Gwaŋo lok (*v*): digress, go off the point,

Gwar (*adj*): coarse

Gwar (*adj*): extraordinary, great, interesting, remarkable, fascinating, attention –grabbing,

Gwar (*adj*): rough, harsh,

Gwar (*adj*): tricky,

Gwar (*adv*): exceptionally,

Gwar (dwan) (*adj*): hoarse, scratchy, ragged,

Gwar agwara (*adj*): husky,

Gwaro (gita) (*v*): strum,

Gweno (*n*): chicken,

Gweno lyec (*n*): turkey,

Gweno ma dako (*n*): hen,

Gweŋ (*n*): rock,

Gweŋ (*v*): kick,

Gwere (*n*): jump, jerk, jolt,

Gwere malo doki piny (*adj*): bumpy,

Gwero bad (*n*): vaccination, immunization,

Gweto (*v*): mark, correct,

Gweto (*v*): tick,

Gweyo (*adj*): repulsive,

Gweyo (*v*): kick,

Gweyo karete (*n*): karate,

Gweyo odilo matek (*v*): drill,

Gwilo lok (ma mite) (*n,leg.*): disclosure,

Gwilo lok (*v*): disclose, reveal,

Gwok (*adj*): caring,

Gwok (*n*): dog, (*adj*), canine

Gwok (*n*): care,

Gwoke (*adj*): careful, cautious, watchful, alert, vigilant, wary, guarded,

Gwoke (*n*): caution, warning, carefulness, care,

Gwoke (*v*): avoid, guard, watch,

Gwoko (*v*): care, cover, protect, keep, own, prevent, store, preserve, maintain, look after, save, put aside, shelter, treat, care for

Gwoko agwoka (doki mar) (*adj*): fatherly

Gwoko ka ciŋ (*v*): stash,

Gwoko ko (*adj*): irresponsible, careless, reckless, negligent,

Gwoko waŋe agwoka (*adj*): strict,

Gwoko waŋe doki kuk kuk (*adj*): motherly, treasured,

Gwoŋ (*n*): stammer, stutter,

I

I (*adv*): about, concerning, in relation to, on the subject of, on, with reference to, as a regards,

I (bas, meli, gar) (*adv*): aboard,

I (bus, meli, gar) (*adj*): aboard,

I (*prep.*): in, on,

I (*prep.*): round,

I (*prep.*): to,

I a conya (*adv*): quaintly,

I a tir ne (*adv*): correctly,

I a tire ko (*adv*): inappropriately,

I acaki me neno ne (*adv*): remarkably,

I ada ne (*adv*): absolutely, actually, affirmatively, certainly, genuinely, indeed, actual, surely, truly, truthfully,

I agiki ne (*adv*): finally, lastly, at last, conclusively, ultimately,

I akoya akoya (*adv*): partially,

I anyim (*adv*): afterward,

I atir ne (*adv*): directly, fairly, genuinely, justly, respectably,

I atura (*adv*): unexpectedly,

I bedo ki cwiny iye (*adv*): enthusiastically,

I bedo maber (*adv*): positively,

I bedo pere (*adv*): presently,

I ber me (*adv*): worthily,

I ber ne (*adv*): respectably,

I bere (*adv*): considerably, significant, substantially,

I bino maber (*adv*): positively,

I bit te (*adv*): sharply, jaggedly,

I bito (*adv*): persuasively,

I bwola - ilibo (*adv*): cunningly,

I caa mukene (*adv*): occasionally,

I caden (*adv*): evidently,

I cani (*adv*): currently,

I cene (*adv*): financially,

I cere cere pa doge (*adv*): jaggedly,

I cik mape tye atir doki petye atir ento tye kakare (*adv*): ethically, morally,

I cime ne (*adv*): impressively,

I ciŋ (*n*): dependent,

I cok cok (*adv*): frequently,

I cok cok ne ko (*adv*): infrequently,

I cwiny (*adj*): personal,

I di (*prep.*): amid,

I dic (*adv*) stressfully,

I didit te (*adv*): substantially,

I dido lok (*adv*): curious, inquisitive, inquiring,

I diŋe ne (*adv*): tightly,

I dite (*adv*): substantially,

I dite makwak (*adv*): enormously,

I ditte (*adv*): considerably, greatly, extensively,

I ducu ne (*adv*): unanimously, universally,

I dwaro ne (*adv*) searchingly,

I dwayo wi dano ki kom lok (*adj*): inappropriately,

I gene ne (*adv*): truthfully,

I gi mu dok yo ikom (*adv*): physically,

I gi na ura madit (*adv*): remarkably,

I gik ne ko (*adv*): infinitely,

I gwar ne (*adv*): roughly,

I ic (*adj*): inward,

I iye (*prep.*): within,

I juko ne (*adv*), reproachfully,

I jwene jwene rye rye (*adv*): instantly,

I jwi jwi ne ko (*adv*): infrequently,

I ka maber (*adv*): safely,

I ka maleŋ (*adv*): officially,

I ka ywe mot (*adv*): restfully,

I kale ne ko (*adv*): inevitably,

I kamaleŋ (*adv*): simply, plainly, well, clearly, visibly,

I kare (*prep.*): during, throughout,

I kare ca ni (*adv*): then, at that time,

I kare eni (*adv*): currently,

I keco (*adv*): icily,

I kelo cuŋo wic mo manok (*adv*): quizzically,

I kido pere mapat (*adv*): extraordinarily,

I kiji kiji (*adv*): thoroughly,

I kin (*n*): paragraph,

I kin (*prep.*): between,

I kin accaki ki agikki me ŋolo kop (*n, leg.*): interlocutory application,

I kin kare (*prep.*): during,

I kit laboŋo nyero mo (*adv*): earnestly,

I kit laboŋo tuko mo (*adv*): earnestly,

I kit ma gi ginywalo kede (*adv*): naturally,

I kit ma jwi ni (*adv*): consistently, constantly, ordinarily, routinely,

I kit ma lare ko (*adv*): indubitably,

I kit ma luloc ŋeyo (*adv*): formally,

I kit ma mede kede (*adv*): continually,

I kit ma ŋol ko (*adv*): constantly,

I kit ma oketo kede (rwom,) (*adv*): structurally,

I kit ma opore (*adv*): ethically, fairly, justly, normally,

I kit ma oyubo kede (*adv*): structurally,

I kit ma pe gi yubo ki iciŋ (*adv*): naturally,

I kit ma twere ko (*adv*): indubitably,

I kit ma yeŋo waŋ dano (*adv*): reasonably,

I kit majwini (*adv*): normally,

I kit mape opore (*adv*): unethical

I kit marac (*adv*): mortally, deadly,

I kit me (tic kede) (*adv*): scientifically, systematically,

I kit me dano adana (*adv*): mortally

I kit me lobo (*adv*): mortally, earthly, wordly,

I kit pa guti ne (*adv*): structurally,

I kit pa lurem (*adv*): warmly,

I kite mapat (*adv*): oddly,

I kome ki kome (*adv*): genuinely, physically,

I konye (*adv*): handily, usefully,

I konyo gin (*adj*): dependent,

I kore ki kore (*adv*): scientifically, systematically,

I kore pa cwiny (*adv*): frentically, anxiously,

I kwanyo kare (*adv*): voluntarily,

I kwe kwe ne (*adv*): lately,

I kwiri ne (*adv*): normally,

I labed naka (*adv*): externally,

I leŋe (coo) (*adv*): handsomely,

I lii ne (*adv*): direct, straight,

I liŋ (pa piny) (*adv*): coolly, serenely, calmly,

I lobo ma woko (*adv*): overseas,

I loc ken (*adv*): independently,

I lok ma longonyo tyene woko (*adv*): paradoxically,

I lweny (*adv*): offensively,

I lwode pa cwiny (*adv*): frentically, anxiously,

I lwoŋo (*adv*): identifiably, name,

I maro ne (*adv*): fondly,

I me bedo gaŋ (boŋo) (*adv*): informally,

I mede ne ameda (*adv*): perpetually,

I medo adaa (*adv*): elaborately,

I medo ŋec (*adv*): elaborately,

I miŋo (*adv*): foolishly, idiotically,

I miyo kom (*adv*): voluntarily,

I miyo tam ni gi mo marac bitime (*adv*): ominously,

I moko iye kiŋ kiŋ (*adv*): persistently,

I moko ne diŋ (*adv*): rigidly,

I muŋ (*adj*): privately, covertly, secretly, stealthily, clandestinely,

I mwonya ne (dako) (*adv*): handsomely,

I nen ne (*adv*): seemingly,

I nen ne (*adv*): visually,

I nen ne cok cok (*adv*): periodically,

I nen ne ko (*adv*): invisibly,

I noŋo (*adv*): identifiably, find,

I nuro (nino) (*adv*): dopily

I nyalo (*adv*): persuasively,

I nyalo dano (*adv*) quaintly,

I nyaŋo (*adv*): elaborately,

I nyero kadi ki lwoŋo (*adv*): hysterically,

I nyote pa kom (*adv*): stressfully,

I ŋabo cwiny (*adv*): tensely,

I ŋe eni (*adv*) then, after that,

I ŋee yo (*adv*) identifiably, spot,

I ŋeno lok (*adv*): offensively,

I ŋete (*adv*): partially,

I ŋeyo kit me lok (*adv*): eloquently,

I ŋic (*adv*): quaintly,

I ŋico (*adv*): icily,

I ŋole ko (*adv*): incessantly,

I ot (*adv*): indoors,

I oyoto yot (*adv*): hastily,

I paŋe ne ko (*adv*): inevitably,

I para (*pron.*): mine,

I patpat ne (*adv*): separately,

I pe ne (*adv*): negatively,

I pe pa cik mape tye atir doki petye atir ento tye kakare (*adv*): unethically,

I pe pa giki ne (*adv*): infinitely,

I pe pa rwate ki lok ma gi tye kaloko ne ni (*adv*): inappropriately,

I pere (*pron.*): his, her, it,

I peri (*pron.*): yours

I pime ne ko (*adv*): immeasurably,

I poke ne (*adv*): separately,

I poko (*adv*): identifiably, distinguish,

I poko ne ko (*adv*): fairly,

I poŋ ki yom cwiny (*adv*): joyfully,

I poŋ ki yomcwiny (*adv*): excitedly,

I poro (*adv*): identifiably, associate,

I poyo wic (*adv*): evocatively,

I pye mot (pa piny) (*adv*): coolly, serenely, calmly,

I race keket ko (*adv*): fairly,

I reme ko (*adv*): painlessly,

I reme makwak (*adv*): painfully,

I rido ne (*adv*): tightly,

I riyo (*adv*): persistently,

I rube pa wic (*adv*): stressfully,

I ryeko –bwola (*adv*): cunningly,

I taco lok (*adv*): frankly,

I tam mayot (*adv*): imaginatively,

I te cik (*adj*): customary, normal,

I te nino eni (*adv*): nowadays,

I te twero (*n*): subject to,

I tedo wic (*adv*): imaginatively,

I tego ne marom (*adv*): harmoniously,

I tek cwiny (*adv*): courageously,

I teŋ (*prep.*): against, along,

I ter (*prep.*): below, under, beneath,

I time ne cok cok (*adv*): periodically,

I timme kalukalu (kom) (*adv*): hysterically,

I tito maber (gimo ma otime ikomi ma ineno ki waŋi) (*adj*): first hand,

I tiyo ki lanen me lakwany (-) (*adv*): negatively,

I tugi (*prons.*): theirs,

I tum ne (*adv*): completely,

I tuŋe pi (*adv*): exclusively, private,

I tuti ko (*adv*): effortless,

I tuwa (*pron.*): ours,

I tuwu (*pron.*): yours,

I twero (*adv*): pontentially,

I twolo ne (*adv*): vacantly,

I tye ne (*adv*): presently,

I tye pere (*adv*): positively,

I tyeko ne (*adv*) completely,

I uc (*adv*): gleefully,

I waco Kamaleŋ (*adv*): expressly,

I waco lok i wic (*adv*): reproachfully,

I waco maber (gimo ma otime ikomi ma ineno ki waŋi) (*adj*): first hand,

I waŋ caa (*adj*): prompt, punctual, promptly,

I waŋ caa ki kome (*adj*): timely, punctually,

I wel ma ka gi poko ki ariyo doŋ acel (*adv*): oddly,

I wel madit ki bot jero (*adv*): positively,

I wel matidi ki bot jero (*adv*): negative,

I weŋ weŋe (*adv*): utterly,

I weŋe (*adv*) unanimously, entirely, fully, generally, normally, universally,

I weŋe ko (*adv*): exclusively, partially,

I wi (*prep.*): at, on,

I wii (bus, meli, gar) (*adv*): aboard,

I winye i kin gi (*adv*): harmoniously,

I wiye wiye (*adv*): superficially,

I wor (*adv*): orderly,

I yenyo (*adv*): identifiably, discover,

I yenyo ne (*adv*) searchingly, shakily,

I yeŋe ne ko (*adv*): steady, stable,

I yot wic (*adv*): imaginatively,

I yub (*adv*): orderly,

Ic (*n*): stomach, womb,

Idi (*adv*): aboard

Idi (*prep.*): among, in the middle of,

Idi iye (*adj*): internal,

Idi yamo (*n*): atmosphere,

Ii (*prep.*): in, inside, into,

Iit dek (*n*): vegetable,

Ikin (ga ariyo) (*adj*): medium,

Ikin (*n*): row,

Ikin (*prep.*): among, between,

Ikin lobo mapatpat (*adj*): international,

Ikin piny (*adj*): heavenly,

Ikin piny (*n*): space, vaccum,

Ikit (calo pa dano) weŋ (*adv*): naturally,

Ikit ma mite (*adv*): accordingly,

Imiti pere (*adj*): discrete,

In (*pron.*): you,

Inyim lwak (*adj*): live,

Iŋe (*adv*): after,

Iŋe (*conj.*): when, after,

Iŋe (*prep.*): after, following,

Iŋe (*prep.*): behind, following,

Iŋe eni (*adv*): afterwards,

Iŋe gi ma pire tek (*adj*): secondary,

Ira (*adj*): personal,

Iritiria (*n*): Eritrea,

It (*n*): ear,

It gwana (*n*): cassava leave,

It yat (*n*): leave,

Ite cik (*adj*): illegal, lawful,

Ite cik (dano weŋ) (*n, leg.*): rule of law,

Ite cik (*n*): legal,

Ite twero (*adj*): liable,

Itere ki kome (*adj*): first hand,

Itipo (*adj*): dark, shady,

Ito (*n*): climb,

Ito (*n*): rise,

Ito (*v*): climb,

Ituwa (*adj*): our,

Iwi (*prep.*): above, onto, on, over, upon,

Iwiye (*prep.*): on,

Iwiye wiye (*adj*): superficial, surface,

Iye (*adj*): content, subject matter, gist, substance (*lit*) inside,

Iye (*adv*): there,

Iye malac (*adv*): extensively, at length, lengthily, broadly,

Iye ŋic (*adj*): generous, kind, liberal, bighearted, openhanded, munificient, giving, charitable,

Iye ocule (*adj*): solid,

J

Jaba (*n*): pocket,

Jaire (*n*): Zaire,

Jake pa ler (*n*): sprain,

Jal (*n*): mate,

Jalo (*v*): slash,

Jami kwaro (*adj*): antique, very old, aged, historic, old – fashioned,

Jami ma itye kede (*n.*): capital, assets, resource,

Jami ma ŋwece kur (*adj*): fragrant,

Jami me lobo (*adj*): mundane,

Jami me lobo ko (*adj*): immaterial,

Jami me tedo (*n*): cutlery,

Jami pa rwode (*n, leg.*): intellectual property,

Janjaru (*n*): bean,

Jany (*v*) radiate,

Jany (yat) (*n*): branch,

Jany yat (*n*): branch of a tree,

Jaŋo kom (*adj*): careless, loose,

Jaŋo kom (*n*): neglect,

Jele (*n*): sway,

Jele (*v*): swing,

Jemo (*n*): rise, rebellion,

Jemo (*v*): rise, rebellion,

Jeŋe (*v*): depend,

Jibi (*n*): buffalo,

Jin (*n*): jean,

Jiŋ (ki ŋico) (*v*): freeze,

Jiŋ (kom) (*adj*): taut,

Jiŋ (*v*): streghten,

Jiŋe (*n*): rise,

Jiŋo (*v*): ice,

Jo gaŋ pa rwodi (*adj*): royal,

Jo ma con (*adj*): ancient,

Jo mi gwoko gin (*adj*): dependent,

Jok (*n*): god, devil

Jokon (*n*): kitchen,

Jol (*adj*): hospitable,

Jol (*n*): cuddle, welcome, hug, embrace, cuddle,

Jol ma malo (*n*): squeeze, cuddle,

Jolo (*v*): hug, embrace, cuddle, hold close,

Jolo (*v*): notice, recognize,

Jolo (*v*): welcome,

Jony (*adj*): lean, thin, skinny, bony,

Jonyo (*adj*): skinny, slim,

Juba (*n*): Juba,

Juk (*n*): ban, rebuke, reproach, reprimand, warning,

Juk (pwony) (*n*): lecture,

Juk pa kot (*n, leg.*): injunction,

Juko (*v*): chide, scold, rebuke, reproach, admonish, reprove, berate, deter, bar, ban, contain, limit,

Jul (*adj*): fiery, fierce, furious, angry,

Jul (*n*): rage,

Jul (*v*): boil, rage, fume,

Junye (*adj*): crowded, teeming,

Jupita (*n*): Jupiter,

Jwaro (wiye) (*adj*): trim,

Jwayo kin lak (*v*): floss,

Jwen (*n*): step, footprint, track,

Jwen (tyelo, ciŋ) (*n*): imprint, stamp,

Jwene jwene rye rye (*adj*): instant,

Jwer (*n*): trim,

Jwero (*n*): cut, slash,

Jwero (*v*): clip, mow, trim,

Jwi jwi (*adj*): frequently, often, regularly, normally, commonly, recurrently, habitually, repeatedly,

Jwi jwi (*adv*): daily, every day, always,

K

Ka (*conj.*): if, whenever, when,

Ka caŋo mon (*n*): gynaecology,

Ka cat ma kelo magoba (*adj*): firm, company,

Ka cel acel (*adj*) rare,

Ka cuŋo pere pe (*adj*): unsteady,

Ka daa (*adj*): detailed, fact,

Ka dikidiki me lok (*n*): point, detail,

Ka i te cik (*adv*): normally, customarily,

Ka kany (*adv*): there, at that point,

Ka kanye (*prep.*): within,

Ka laŋeti (*adj*): neighbour,

Ka lim cokcok (*n*): haunt,

Ka maber (*adj*): safe,

Ka maber ko (*adj*): dangerous, unsafe, treacherous, perilous,

Ka maleŋ (*adj*): official,

Ka maleŋ (*adv*): explicitly,

Ka maleŋ (Nyuto nyim) (*adv*): explicitly,

Ka me gwoko cene (*n*): account, bank,

Ka me gwoko ga (*n*): store,

Ka me gwoko ga me mwony (*n*): dump,

Ka me gwoko lim (*n*): account, bank,

Ka me tweyo meli (*n*): dock,

Ka me wilo yat (*n*): chemist,

Ka me yubo ga (*n*): plant, factory,

Ka mo keken (*conj.*): wherever, to any place,

Ka noŋe (*n*): contact, address,

Ka odwoko yo tuŋ cel (*prep.*): against, in contradiction,

Ka pime (*n*): medical,

Ka pudi tye (*conj.*): as long as,

Ka rweyo tyelo bot dano weŋ (*n*): park,

Ka tere pe (*adj*): vain, ineffective, useless, hopeless, unproductive, futile, abortive, worthless, unsuccessful,

Ka tire pe (*adj*): vague,

Ka too pa ceŋ (*n*): West,

Ka tum ne (*adv*): finally, lastly, at last, conclusively,

Ka tum pa nino (*n, leg.*): sunset clauses,

Kaa (*n*): car,

Kabat (*n*): cupboard,

Kabedo (*n*): contact,

Kabedo (*v*): live, reside,

Kabic (*n*): cabbage,

Kac (*n*): bite,

Kac (*n*): yield, harvest,

Kac (*v*): harvesting,

Kacel (*adv*): together,

Kacel ki (*prep.*): plus,

Kaciŋe (*adv*): aside,

Kacoke (*n*): meeting, conference, meeting, gathering, function,

Kacuŋo (*n*): point, instant, stand, attitude,

Kacuŋo me lok (*n*): point, position,

Kadi (*adv*): even,

Kadi ... (*conj.*): either...

Kadi ... (*Conj.*): neigther ...

Kadi bedi (*conj.*): although, though, even though, even if, while, wether,

Kadi bedi (*prep.*): despite,

Kado (*n*): salt,

Kaka (*n*): place, location, spot, place,

Kaka (*n*): point, position,

Kaka me tic (*n*): post, postion,

Kakare (*adj*): right, correct, true, accurate, exact, precise, appropriate, apt, suitable, fitting, authentic, genuine, real, valid, reliable, dependable, realistic, definite, exact, indisputable, unadulterated, legitimate, valid, actual, judicious, proper,

Kakare (*n*): map,

Kakare (otimo ki cwiny weŋ) (*adj*): rigorous,

Kakare ko (*adj*): wrong, incorrect, mistaken, erroneous,

Kaketo cik (*n, leg.*): parliament,

Kala ma patpat (*adj*): colorful,

Kalwok (*v*): bath,

Kama bor (*adj*): faraway,

Kama bor wa idi caro (*adj*): far –flung, remote,

Kama ciŋ ok iye (*adj*): dangerous, unsafe

Kama cok (*adj*): handy, near, nearby, convenient, within reach, close, accessible, manageable, at hand,

Kama ogule (*n*): bend, curve,

Kama rac (*adj*): dangerous, unsafe,

Kamaleŋ (*adj*) clear, apparent, lucid, plain, obvious, comprehensible, patent, transparent, bare, (*lit.*) in open place, blank, empty, frank, honest, handy, near, nearby, convenient, within reach, close, accessible, manageable, at hand, honest, open, direct, obvious, visible,

Kamaleŋ (*adv*): openly,

Kame kano ga (calo cene) (*n*): stash,

Kame poyo wic (*adj*): monument,

Kamo keken (*adv*): elsewhere,

Kamo macon me poyo wic (*adj*): monument,

Kampala (*n*): Kampala,

Kane (*n*): cover, disguise,

Kane (*v*): bury, hide, cover, conceal, shelter, take shelter,

Kane rac (*adj*): dangerous, hairy,

Kanica (*n*): church,

Kany (*adv*): here,

Kany (*adv*): there, at that point,

Kany (*adv*): where,

Kany (*n*): point, position,

Kany (*pre*: *tye*) (*adv*): around,

Kany (ru) (*adv*): much,

Kapok (*n*): tilapia,

Karatac me coc (*n*): pad, notebook,

Karaton (*n*): box,

Kare (*n*): span,

Kare (*n*): time,

Kare ducu (*adj*): all the time, daily, numerous, frequent, many, several,

Kare ducu ko (*adv*): seldom, rarely,

Kare eni (*adj*): current, present,

Kare macek (*adj*): short –term, temporary,

Kare manok (*adj*): temporary, short- term,

Kare mapol (*adj*): several, mumerous, quite a lot,

Kare me tic (*n*): shift, period,

Karot (*n*): carrot,

Kartum (*n*): Khartoum,

Katino (*n*): childhood,

Katir (*adj*): detailed, fact,

Katir ma ŋolo kop cuŋ iye (*n, leg.*): ration decidendi,

Katire (*adj*): detailed,

Kato (*prep.*): above, more than, over, past,

Kato (*v*): exceed

Kato (*v*): pass,

Kato ko (*v*): fail, not pass,

Katuko (*n*): park,

Katum ciŋ (*adv*): aside,

Katum ciŋa/wa (*adj*): aboard, on board, on our side,

Katyelo (*n*): step,

Kayo (*v*): bite,

Kec (*adj*): bitter,

Kec (*adj*): hungry,

Kec (*adj*): selfish, ungenerous

Keco (*adj*): angry, uptight, bitter,

Keco (*n*): anger,

Keco (*v*): anger, annoy, rage, enrage, madden, infuriate, irritate,

Keken (*adj*): only,

Keken (*adv*): just,

Keken (*adv*): merely, only,

Keken ni (*adv*): simply,

Keko it (*adj*): alert,

Keko it (*n*): alert,

Keko it (*n*): warning, caution, attention,

Keko it (*v*): alert, attentive, warn, caution,

Kelkel (*adj*): sparse,

Kelo (*v*): bring,

Kelo (*v*): introduce, bring in,

Kelo cuŋo wic mo manok (*adj*): quizzical,

Kelo kom (*v*): report, turn up,

Kelo kumo (*adj*): dismal,

Kelo lworo (*adj*): scary, horrible, creepy, threatening, scare,

Kelo lworo (*v*): scare,

Kelo magoba (*adj*): profitable,

Kelo par (*adj*): worrisome,

Kelo par (*v*): gnaw, cause worry,

Kemo (*n*): march, advanced,

Kemo (*n*): object, target,

Kemo (*v*): direct, aim,

Ken (*adj*): single,

Kene (*adj*): lonely, lone,

Kenya (*n*): Kenya

Keŋ (*v*): miss, fail to attend,

Kero (*n*): force, power, drive, energy, push, grasp, ability to do something,

Kero kom (*n*): alert, guard,

Kero pere pe (*adj*): powerless,

Kero pere pe (bot dano) (*adj*): frail, weak, fragile, delicate, in poor health,

Ket (*n*): divorce, separation,

Ket (*v*): divorce,

Keti (*adj*): attached, (lit) put,

Keto (di gi begu) (*v*): unpack,

Keto (*v*): enter, insert, include,

Keto (*v*): form, set something up,

Keto (*v*): paste, place, plant, put, set,

Keto (*v*): scatter,

Keto (yer): comb, untangle,

Keto cal (*v*): frame,

Keto cen (*v*): stow,

Keto cene (*v*): invest,

Keto cik (*n, leg.*): legislation,

Keto cik (*v*): stipulate,

Keto cik macek (*v*): enunciate,

Keto cwiny (*adj*): determined,

Keto cwiny (*adj*): envious,

Keto cwiny (*adj*): focused,

Keto cwiny (*adj*): personal,

Keto cwiny (*v*): wish,

Keto cwiny iga (*n*): envy, jelousy,

Keto cwiny iye (*v*): note, notice,

Keto cwiny iye ko (*adv*): absentmindedly,

Keto cwiny iye ko (*v*): ignore,

Keto gen iye weŋ (*adv*): overconfident,

Keto i di waŋ kor (*v*): frame,

Keto idi bok (*v*): box,

Keto idi yamo (*v*): broadcast, transmit,

Keto itic (*v*): exercise, put into effect, practice, employs,

Keto iwic (*v*): remember,

Keto ka maleŋ (*v*): release, stipulate, specify,

Keto ka waŋe (*v*): replace, susbstitute,

Keto kacel (*v*): nest,

Keto Ki giŋi me pii (*v*): dam,

Keto kit me tic ki cik i machine (*v*): program,

Keto lanen (*v*): label, mark,

Keto lewic (*adj*): humiliating, mortified,

Keto lewic (*v*): disappoint, upset, embarrass, fail, disappoint, shame,

Keto lworo (*adj*): alarming, alarm,

Keto lworo (*v*): frighten, scare,

Keto lworo i cwiny (*adj*): scared, frightened, terrified, timid, petrified,

Keto ne itic (*n*): exercise, implementation,

Keto piny (*v*): down, put down,

Keto piny taŋ taŋ (*v*): sack, ransack,

Keto pire matek (*v*): emphasize, value,

Keto pire matek (*v*): matter,

Keto tam (*v*): concentrate,

Keto waŋ i yoo (*v*): pine, yearn,

Keto waŋ matwolo (*v*): guard,

Keto wele (*v*): cost, number, rate, value,

Ki (*prep.*): among, with, by, through, down, along, from, as of,

Ki (*prep.*): than,

Ki (*prep.*): versus,

Ki (*prep.*): via,

Ki a dunno ne weŋ (*adv*): heartily,

Ki aber ne (*adv*): ironically,

Ki acakki ne ki agiki ne pe (*adv*): immensely,

Ki acel acel (*adv*) rarely, seldom,

Ki adaa ne (*adv*): sincerely, genuinely, truthfully,

Ki akalakala (*adv*): doubtfully, questioningly, suspiciously,

Ki akalakala peke iye (*adv*): positively,

Ki akoda (*adv*): humorously, playfully,

Ki apir (*adv*): grudgingly,

Ki apopora (*adv*): dramatically,

Ki apoya (*adv*): zanily,

Ki aranyi (*adv*): brutally,

Ki arii arii (*adv*): diagonally,

Ki aura (*adv*): spectacularly,

Ki bako ne (*adv*): presumably,

Ki bal (*adv*): wrongly,

Ki bedo ki ŋec (*adv*): knowlegeably,

Ki bedo macan can (*adv*): miserably,

Ki ber kit (*adv*): generously,

Ki ber kit (*adv*): tenderly,

Ki bere (*adv*): compactly, well, efficiently, favourably, siginificantly,

Ki bero (*adv*): decently, generously, loftily, nicely,

Ki bino (pere) iwic (*adv*): hauntingly,

Ki bita (*adv*): coaxingly,

Ki boma (*adv*): sly,

Ki boŋo boŋo (*adv*): materially,

Ki boro ne (*adv*): vertically,

Ki bot kom (*adv*): lazily,

Ki bura (*adv*): darkly, menacingly,

Ki cac (*adv*): defiant, disobedient, insolent, judgmentally, naughtily,

Ki can (*adv*): needily, poorly,

Ki caricari (*adv*): clumsily,

Ki caro (*adv*): carelessly, recklessly, shoddily,

Ki cere (*adv*): daringly,

Ki cero ne (*adv*): markedly,

Ki cil cwiny (*adv*): bravely,

Ki ciŋ ko (*adv*): mechanincally,

Ki ciŋ ma yot (*adv*): deftly,

Ki cok cwinye (*adv*): emotionally,

Ki col cwiny (*adv*): cruelly, viciously,

Ki col ripiripi (*adv*): dimly,

Ki cora acora (*adv*): clumsily,

Ki cuko (cwiny) (*adv*): promptly,

Ki cuŋo wic (*adv*): puzzling,

Ki cuŋo wii dano (*adv*): confusedly,

Ki cwer cwiny (*adv*): touchingly,

Ki cwiny makwar (*adv*): unkindly,

Ki cwiny maŋic (*adv*): kindly,

Ki cwiny marac (*adv*): coldly,

Ki cwiny weŋ (*adv*): earnestly,

Ki cwiny weŋ (*adv*): sincerely, honestly,

Ki cwiny weŋ (*adv*): warmly, solemnly,

Ki cwinye iye (*adv*): eagerly,

Ki cwinye weŋ (*adv*): heartily, believably, whole – heatedly,

Ki cwinye weŋ iye (*adv*): admiringly, affectionately, admiringly, affectionately,

Ki deyo (*adv*): gracefully, majestically, stylishly,

Ki dikdik ko (tic) (*adv*): casually,

Ki dilo ne (*adv*): compactly, not wastefully, economically,

Ki diri (*adj*): formal,

Ki diri (*adv*): diligently, subtly,

Ki diri doki rwom (*adv*): solemnly,

Ki dit ne (*adv*): vastly,

Ki ditte makwak ni (*adv*): hugely,

Ki ditte maloyo weŋ ni (*adv*): greatly,

Ki diyo cwiny (*adv*): patiently,

Ki dwan ma malo (*adv*): loudly,

Ki dwiro (*adv*): speedily,

Ki ga (*adv*): materially,

Ki ga pa lolonyo (*adv*): luxuriously,

Ki gemo (*adv*): fatally,

Ki gen (*adv*): faithfully, reliably,

Ki gen ma tye kede (*adv*): optimistically,

Ki gen weŋ (*adv*): sincerely, honestly,

Ki gene ko (*adv*): dangerously,

Ki gero (*adv*): ferociously, violently, cruelly, fiercely, ruthless, viciously,

Ki gero (pa le tim) (*adv*): viciously,

Ki gi mi lobo (*adv*): materially,

Ki gi mo iwic (*adv*): crazy, illogically, witlessly, frantically, eccentrically,

Ki gi mo tye i wiye (*adv*): frantically,

Ki giŋi (*adv*): judgementally, strictly, subtle,

Ki giŋi (me pii) (*n*): dam,

Ki giŋi (*n*): bar, obstruction,

Ki giŋi idok kulu (*n*): barrage,

Ki goro (*adv*): weakly,

Ki goro lok ikome (*adv*): suspiciously,

Ki goro pere (*adv*): delicately

Ki gum kom (*adv*): fortunately, luckily, thankfully, luckily,

Ki gum kom ma pe (*adv*): unfortunately,

Ki gware (*adv*): interestingly,

Ki gwaro (pere ni) (*adv*): harshly,

Ki gwetone (*adv*): markedly,

Ki gwoke (*adv*): carefully, cautiously,

Ki i (*prep.*): from, as of,

Ki i adda ne (*adv*): honestly,

Ki i atir (*adv*): honestly,

Ki i cwiny (*adv*): inwardly, personally,

Ki i di (*prep.*): along,

Ki i diri (*adv*): formally,

Ki i ot yat (*adv*): medically

Ki i pime (ot yat) (*adv*): medically,

Ki i te cik, ikit ma pe rac nyo ber (*adv*): morally,

Ki ic (*adv*): inwardly,

Ki idi iye (*adv*): internally,

Ki ira (*adv*): personally,

Ki jaŋo kom ne (*adv*): loosely,

Ki jiŋe ko (*adv*): limply,

Ki jul (*adv*): furiously,

Ki ka ma ber ko (*adv*): dangerously,

Ki kala mapat pat (*adv*): colourfully,

Ki Kama ciŋ ok iye (*adv*): dangerously,

Ki kamaleŋ (*adv*): honestly, clearly,

Ki Kamarac (*adv*): dangerously,

Ki Kec (*adv*): hungrily,

Ki kec (*adv*): meanly, selfishly,

Ki kec ko (*adv*): unselfishly,

Ki keco (*adv*): bitterly, resentfully, acrimoniously, sulkily, sullenly, cynical, angrily, indignantly,

Ki keco (*adv*): crossly, furiously, resentfully,

Ki kero (*adv*): powerfully,

Ki keto lworo i cwiny (*adv*): scarily,

Ki keto ne cwiny (*adv*): markedly,

Ki kica (*adv*): compassionately, sympathetically,

Ki kit ma opore (*adv*): morally,

Ki kom ma yila ayila (*adv*): eagerly,

Ki kom ma yila ayila (*adv*): impatiently,

Ki kome ma myela amyela (*adv*): eagerly,

Ki kome ne mutto ma ŋeyo ko (*adv*): numbly,

Ki kony (*adv*): helpfully,

Ki kony ne (*adv*): favourably,

Ki kony pere (*adv*): efficiently, effectively, usefully, helpfully,

Ki kuc (*adv*): comfortably, enjoyably,

Ki kumu (*adv*): darkly,

Ki kur (*adv*): vigilantly,

Ki kuro ne (*adv*): longingly,

Ki kwar cwiny (*adv*): cruelly,

Ki kwer (*adv*): jubilaintly,

Ki kwero cwiny (*adv*): hatefully,

Ki lace (*adv*): widely,

Ki ladwe (*adv*): monthly,

Ki laro ne (*adv*): hurriedly,

Ki lelek (*adv*): dreamily,

Ki leŋ cwiny (*adv*): generously,

Ki leŋ kom (*adv*): healthily,

Ki leŋ waŋ (*adv*): generously,

Ki leŋe ko (bot mon) (*adv*): plainly,

Ki leŋo (*adv*): cleanly,

Ki leŋo (*adv*): prettily,

Ki lewic keken (*adv*): outrageously,

Ki lime (*adv*): sweetly,

Ki liŋ ne (*adv*): silently,

Ki lit kom (*adv*): queasily,

Ki liu ne (dwan) (*adv*): shrilly,

Ki loc (*adv*) victoriously,

Ki loc weŋ (*adv*): mighty,

Ki lowade (*adv*): aboard, on the team, on the project

Ki lwodo cwiny (*adv*): nervously, suspiciously,

Ki lworo (*adv*): cowardly,

Ki malo (*adv*): highly,

Ki malo (*adv*): upwardly,

Ki mani (*adv*): innocently, sheepishly, shyly,

Ki maŋ (*adv*): crazily, madly,

Ki maŋ (*adv*): madly,

Ki mar (*adv*): generously, lovingly, warmly,

Ki maro peny (*adv*): inquisitively,

Ki miŋo (*adv*): ridiculously, stupidly,

Ki mit kom (*adv*): busily, exceitedly, agitatedly, anxiously, vehemently, enthuasiastically, zealously, jauntily, lively,

Ki mit kom me kwan (*adv*): studiously,

Ki mite ko makwak (*adv*): obnoxiuosly,

Ki miti (*adv*): yearningly,

Ki miti (mar, rwate, timo gin moni) (*adv*): passionately,

Ki miti iye (*adv*): keenly,

Ki miyo kom (*adv*): faithfully, oblingingly,

Ki moko ijwen (*adv*): loyally,

Ki mono pere (*adv*): delicately

Ki mowolo ne (*adv*): docilely,

Ki muŋ (*adv*): darkly, mysteriously,

Ki mwolo (*adv*): gently, shyly,

Ki myelo kom (*adv*): scarily,

Ki nede nede pere (*adv*): lithely,

Ki nino nino (*adv*): sleepily,

Ki niyee (*adv*): willingly,

Ki noke (*adv*): scarcely,

Ki nyaŋ (*adv*): silicitiously,

Ki nyaŋo (*adv*): considerately,

Ki nyate (*adv*): vainly,

Ki nyeko (*adv*): jealously,

Ki nyobe pere (*adv*): disorderly,

Ki nyonyo (*adv*): mechanically,

Ki nyune (*adv*): densely,

Ki ŋala (*adv*): mockingly,

Ki ŋec (*adv*): compactly, professionally, knowingly, skillfully,

Ki ŋeno cwiny (*adv*): irritably, rudely,

Ki ŋeto cwiny (*adv*): nastily, outrageously,

Ki ŋic ic (*adv*): generously,

Ki ŋole ko (*adv*): invariably,

Ki ŋoyo laa (*adv*): interestingly,

Ki ŋunde (*adv*): resentfully,

Ki oolo (*adv*): wearily,

Ki oyot oyot (*adv*): promptly,

Ki par (*adv*): worriedly,

Ki patpat (*adv*): differently,

Ki peke pa ŋole (*adv*): invariably,

Ki pekke (*adv*): heavily,

Ki pime (ne) (*adv*): measurably,

Ki piro ne (*adv*): begrudgingly,

Ki pwoc (*adv*): gratefully, thankfully,

Ki pwol pwol (*adv*): cloudily,

Ki pwony (*adv*): uplifingly,

Ki pwote (*adv*): smoothly,

Ki pye mot (*adv*): calmly,

Ki rac cwiny (*adv*) ruthlessly,

Ki rac kit (*adv*): harshly, rudely,

Ki raco (*adv*): dastardly, fatally, wickedly,

Ki raco ne ni (*adv*): grimly,

Ki rep pelpel (*adv*): daintily,

Ki rep pere (*adv*): delicately,

Ki rubo wic (*adv*): puzzling,

Ki rubo wii dano (*adv*): confusedly,

Ki rwom mamalo (*adv*): loftily,

Ki rwom pere mapiny (*adv*): poorly,

Ki ryeko (*adv*): cleverly, brilliantly, giftedly, skillfully, intelligently, wisely,

Ki taco lok (*adv*): candidly,

Ki tam (*adv*): intently,

Ki tam iye (*n, leg.*): discretion,

Ki tamo lok ikom (*adv*): suspiciously,

Ki tek cwiny (*adv*): bravely, valiantly,

Ki tek wic (*adv*): boldly, presumably,

Ki teko (*adv*): intensely, mightily, powerfully, strenuously,

Ki tere tere (*adv*): regularly,

Ki tere tere ko (*adv*): irregular,

Ki tino tino (*adv*): childishly,

Ki tude ne (*adv*): knottily,

Ki tur pere oyot (*adv*): delicately

Ki turo cwiny (*adv*): poignantly,

Ki turo ne atura (*adv*): bewilderedly,

Ki twolo waŋ (*adv*): vigilantly,

Ki tyene (*adv*): meaningfully,

Ki tyer pere oyot (a*dv*): delicately,

Ki ur (*adv*): magically, (*adv*): singularity, startlingly, surprisingly, unbelievably, wonderfully,

Ki ur madit (*adv*): brilliantly, marvellously, wonderfully, excellently, magnificiently, superbly, splendidly, astonishingly,

Ki wac kom (*adv*): lazily,

Ki wake (*adv*): boastfully, immodestly, arrogantly, conceitedtly, loftily, proudly,

Ki wano (*adv*): dangerously,

Ki wic matiyo ko (*adv*): kookily,

Ki winy (*adv*): obediently,

Ki winye ko (*adv*): defiantly

Ki winye ma pe (*adv*): defiantly,

Ki woko (*adv*): externally, outwardly,

Ki woo (*adv*): noisily,

Ki woro (*adv*): affectionately, affectionately, certainly, decently, greedily, politely, respectfully,

Ki ye waŋ (*adv*): interestingly,

Ki yeŋo cwiny (*adv*): scarily,

Ki yo woko (*adv*): outwardly,

Ki yoge ne (*adv*): loosely,

Ki yom cwiny (*adv*): brightly, cheerfully, happily, colorfully, generously, impressively, interestingly, jovially, kindheartedly, merrily, nicely,

Ki yome (*adv*): softly,

Ki yomo cwiny (*adv*) delightful,

Ki yot kom (*adv*): energetically, healthily, lively,

Ki yub (*adv*): neatly,

Ki yweka (*adv*): famously,

Kic (*n*): bees,

Kica (*adj*): compassionate, sympathetic, kind, empathetic, considerate, kindhearted,

Kickic (*adj*): abject, miserable, wretched, dismal,

Kicwica (*n*): cook leave of pumpkin,

Kidi (*n*): rock,

Kido (*n*): form, shape,

Kido pere pat (*adj*): quaint, strange, peculiar, odd, bizarre, weird, extraordinary, unusual,

Kido pere pe (*adj*) ugly, unsightly, colorless, dull,

Kido pere rac (*adj*): ugly, horrible, dreadful, horrid, unsightly,

Kijikiji (*adj*): thorough,

Kijiko (*n*): spoon,

Kila (*adj*): every,

Kila (*adv*): every,

Kila caa (*adv*): hourly,

Kila cabit (*adj*): weekly,

Kila dwe (*adj*): monthly,

Kila mwaka (*adj*): yearly,

Kila mwaka (*adv*): yearly,

Kila wor (*adv*): nightily,

Kin (*adj*): distant,

Kin agiki (*n*): span,

Kin kare me cobo - i kwo pa ŋat mo keken (*adj*): prime,

Kincaca (*n*): Kinshasa,

Kiniga (*adj*): wrath, anger, fury, rage, angry, uptight,

Kiraka (*adj*): ragged,

Kiro (*v*): spray,

Kit (*adj*): habit, manner,

Kit (calo pa dano) weŋ (*adj*): natural,

Kit (Mutukari) (*n*): make, brand,

Kit (*n*): brand, type, breed, form, make,

Kit (*n*): practice, custom,

Kit (*n*): status, lifestyle,

Kit (pa gi moni) (*n*): stamp,

Kit atir (*adj*): upright, righteous,

Kit atir (*n, leg.*): equity,

Kit ber (*adj*): generous, kind, liberal, bighearted, openhanded, munificent, giving, charitable, good –natured, tender, kind,

Kit ma gi ginywalo (i) kede (*adj*): natural,

Kit ma gi keto icik (*adj*): legitimate, lawful,

Kit ma jo ma woto kiyeya nyo meli pimo ki piny (*adj*): nautical,

Kit ma jwi (*adj*), common, everyday,

Kit ma jwi ni (*adj*): normal, usual, regular, ordinary, conventional, typical, traditional, routine,

Kit ma jwi ni ko (*adj*): unsual, unconvential, offbeat, uneven, not regular, not consisitent,

Kit ma jwijwi ni (*adv*): usually,

Kit ma lotimo kede (*n*): form, procedure,

Kit ma mite ko (*adj*): abnormal, nonstandard,

Kit ma oketo kede (*adj*): structural,

Kit ma opore (*adj*): ethical, moral,

Kit ma oyubo kede (*adj*): structural,

Kit macon (*adj*): classic,

Kit magi moko icik (*adj*): legitimate, legal,

Kit me (tic kede**)** (*adj*): scientific, technical, methodological, systematical, logical, precise,

Kit me ŋwido lok i dul (ikin loŋol kop) (*n, leg.*): docket system,

Kit me poko cako winyo lok idi kot (*n, leg.*): cause of action,

Kit me timo ne (*n*): procedure,

Kit pa dako (*adj*): feminine,

Kit rac (*adj*): fithy, wicked, corrupt, dishonest,

Kite con kumenu (*adj*): natural,

Kite kelo nyero (*adj*): abnormal, funny,

Kite pat (*adj*): unusual, strange, odd, extraodrdinary, abnormal, remarkable, bizarre, typical, aloof, indifferent, cold, crooked, weird, peculiar, quirky,

Kite pat (*adv*): quirkily,

Kite pat apata (*adj*): special,

Kite pat ko (*adj*): ordinary,

Kite pe (*adj*): abnormal, uncharacteristic, atypical,

Kite pe atir (*adj*): dishonest, filthy, wicked, corrupt,

Kite pe tye (calo pa dano) **weŋ** (*adj*): unnatural,

Kite rac (*adj*): unkind, cruel, harsh, creepy,

Kite tye kumeno (*adj*): normal, natural,

Kitungulu (*n*): onion,

Kiyo (*n*): glass,

Kiyo (*v*): stay, wait,

Ko (*adv*): not,

Kobe (*n*) migration,

Kobe (*n*): move, shift,

Kobe (*v*): move, change,

Kobe i lobo mukene (*v*): emigrate,

Kobo (*v*): move, switch, change, shift, transfer, copy, evacuate,

Kodi (*n*): seed,

Kodo cwiny (*adj*): stimulating,

Kok (dyaŋ) (*v*): bellow,

Kok (maloŋo calo pa muduku) (*n*): bang,

Kok (*n*): call, cry, lament, crying,

Kok (pa ogwal) (*v*): croak,

Kok (telepon) (*n*): buzz,

Kok (*v*): cry, lament,

Kok (*v*): sound,

Kok ki cwer cwiny (*n*): wail,

Kok ki cwer cwiny (*v*): wail,

Kok ki dwan maliu (doŋo oduru) (*v*) screech,

Kok ki dwan maliu (*n*): yelp,

Kok ki dwan maliu (*v*): yelp,

Kok laliŋ (*adj*): muffled,

Kok laliŋ (*n*): whimper,

Kok laliŋ (*v*): whimper,

Kok maloŋo (calo pa telepone) (*adj*) Buzzing,

Koki lwet (*n*): nail,

Koko (calo tula) (*n*): hoot,

Koko (dwan telepon) (*adj*): humming,

Koko (*n*): sob,

Koko pa a kuru (*adj*): cooing,

Koko pa dyaŋ (*n*): below,

Koko pa muduku (*n*): barrage,

Koko pa ogwal (*n*): croak,

Koko pa twol (*adj*): hissing,

Koko too (*v*): mourn,

Kom (*adj*): practical,

Kom (*n*): body,

Kom (*n*): chair,

Kom (*n*): frame, body,

Kom (*v*): limp,

Kom ada (*adj*): tangible,

Kom bot (*adj*): lazy,

Kom lok (*adj*): sure,

Kom lok ki kome (*adv*): surely,

Kom ma bulubulu (*n*): bloom,

Kom ma onyote (*adj*): wobbly, feeling weak,

Kome bilibili (*adj*): lean,

Kome dit (*adj*): mammoths

Kome doki yer (*adj*): hairy,

Kome gum ko (*adj*): unlucky, ill-fated, unlucky, unfortunate, wretched, miserable, luckless,

Kome gwar (*adj*): granular,

Kome kamaleŋ (*adv*): physically,

Kome ki kome (*adj*): orginal, physical, genuine, real, authentic, indisputable, true, unadulterated, legitimate, valid, actual, pristine, tangible,

Kome ki kome (*adv*): sincerely, really,

Kome ki kome ko (*adj*): fake, virtual,

Kome leŋ (*adj*): healthy, hearty, robust,

Kome mit (*adj*): active, perky,

Kome myela amyela (*adj*): eager,

Kome ne otto ŋeyo ko (*adj*): numb,

Kome ogwade (*adj*): scratched, damaged,

Kome omute (*adj*): damaged, hurt,

Kome pek (*adj*) sturdy,

Kome yila ayila (*adj*): eager, impatient, excited, jumpy,

Kome yot (*adj*): healthy, athletic, fit, sporty, in good shape, physical, agile, nimble, muscular, vigorous, agile, deafening, boisterous, energetic, lively,

Kongo (*n*): Congo,

Kono (*prep.*): save, but, except,

Kono laboŋo (*prep.*): excepting, except,

Kony (*n*): assist, favour, help, support, backing, provision,

Kony pere pe (*adj*): unfit, useless, immaterial,

Konye matek (*n*): constipation,

Konye pe (*adj*): inferior, substandard, negligible, insiginificant, petty, pitiful, pointless, puny, useless, meaningless, poor, weak,

Konyo (*adj*): helpful, useful, favourable , advantageous, instructive, useful, supportive, helpful, practical, fuctional, of use, constructive, positive, valuable, handy, nifty, effective, informative, convenient, expedient, beneficial, worthwile, back, sponsor, support, assist, finance, (*lit.*) help, productive,

Konyo (*adv*): compact, effectively,

Konyo (*v*): assert, defend,

Konyo (*v*): encourage, support, favour, help, assist,

Konyo adada (*adj*): helpful,

Konyo ko (*adj*): helpless, damaging, unhelpful, negative,

Konyo kome kwe (*adj*): defenseless, helpless

Konyo kome wa (*adj*): responsible,

Konyo kor (*adj*): assured, assurance,

Konyo kor (*v*): weigh,

Konyo makulu (*adj*): helpful,

Konyo makwak (*adj*): helpful,

Koŋ (*n*): knock,

Koŋo (*n*): alcohol,

Koŋo (*v*): Knock,

Kop (*n*): concern, finding, judgement,

Kor (*n*): track, path, road,

Kor (*n*): chest,

Kor boŋo pa mon (*n*): blouse,

Kor yat (*n*): stem,

Kore (tye, pe) (*adj*): subtle,

Kore ki kore (*adj*): scientific, technical, methodological, systematical, logical, precise, definitive,

Kore ki kore (*adv*): methodically,

Kore pek (*adj*): burly, gigantic, hefty,

Korton (*n*): box,

Kot (*n*): rain,

Kot ma obolo dog iye (*n, leg.*): appellate courts,

Kot mucwe ki yamo (*n*): storm,

Koyo (*adj*): partial, alienated,

Koyo (*v*): omit,

Koyo ko (*adj*): impartial,

Kubaya (*n*): cup,

Kubo (*v*): connect,

Kubo dog (*n*): quote, quotation,

Kuc (*adj*): peaceful, pleasurable, delightful, blissful, enjoyable,

Kuc (*n*): peace, order, treat,

Kuca (*adj*): there,

Kuca (*adv*): there, in or that place,

Kulekule (*n*): preschool,

Kulo (*n*): river,

Kulu (*adj*): whole,

Kumo (*adj*): anguished, down, depressed, distressed, tormented, agonized, grief-stricken, sorrowful, glum, soulful,

Kumo (*v*): lament, mourn,

Kun (*adj*): grumpy,

Kun (*n*): sulk,

Kun (*v*): protest,

Kur (*adj*): vigilant, watchful,

Kur (*n*): wait, watch,

Kura (*n*): alert,

Kuro (*adj*): longing,

Kuro (*adv*): waiting,

Kuro (lweny) (*adj*): defensive,

Kuro (*v*) bear, put up with, expect, wait for,

Kuro (*v*): bake,

Kuro (*v*): savour, relish,

Kuro (*v*): watch, guard,

Kute (i loko leb) (*n*): command,

Kuto (*v*): blow, sound, ring out,

Kuto buruzi (Arabiya) (*n*): hoot,

Kuto cwiny (*v*): crave,

Kuyere (*n*): spare, standby,

Kwac (*n*) claim, demand, call, request, appeal,

Kwale (*adj*): stealthy,

Kwale akwala (*adv*): stealthily,

Kwalo akwala (*v*): elope,

Kwan (*n*): count,

Kwano (*adj*): calculating, scholarly,

Kwano (*v*): count,

Kwano (*v*): read,

Kwano caa (*v*): time,

Kwano leta (*v*): spell,

Kwano tam (*n*): psychology,

Kwano tyeŋ nyo buk matito pilok mo (*adj*): poetic,

Kwany (*n*): pick,

Kwany (*v*): remove, take

Kwanyo (*n*): release, relief,

Kwanyo (*v*): cut, pick, remove, take off, snatch, take,

Kwanyo (*v*): sack, dismiss,

Kwanyo ga (*v*): produce, take something out,

Kwanyo kare (*adj*): voluntary,

Kwanyo me tek kom (*v*): usurp,

Kwanyo oyot oyot (*v*): swoop,

Kwaŋ (*adj*): buoyant, swim,

Kwaŋ (*v*): float, sail, glide,

Kwar (*adj*): red,

Kwar cwiny (*adj*): cruel,

Kwar marmar (*adj*): pink,

Kwar yelo yelo (*adj*): orange,

Kwaro (*n*): grand father,

Kwaro madit (*n*): great grand father,

Kwayo (*v*): beg, request, pray, implore, plead,

Kwayo (*v*): urge,

Kwayo kica (*v*): apologize,

Kwe (*adj*): late,

Kwe (*adv*): late,

Kwena (*n*): press,

Kwer (*adj*): celebration, jubilaint,

Kwer (*n*): dislike, rebuff, rejection, aversion, hatred,

Kwer (*n*): menstruating, period,

Kwer (*n*): ritual, initiation,

Kwer (*n, leg.*): rites,

Kwere ko (*adv*): irrefutably,

Kweri (*n*): hoe,

Kwero (*adj*): celebrated,

Kwero (*adj*): unwilling, reluctance,

Kwero (*v*): deny, dislike, object, rebuff, reject, refused,

Kwero (*v*): mark, celebrate,

Kwero cwiny (*adj*): hateful, abhorrent, distasteful, disgusting, detestable,

Kwero cwiny (*n*): hate,

Kwero cwiny (*v*): hate, abhor,

Kweyo (arem) (*v*): soothe,

Kweyo (*v*): brake, slow,

Kweyo (*v*): calm, subdue, comfort,

Kweyo cwiny (*n*): comfort,

Kweyo cwiny (*v*): advise,

Kweyo kom (*adj*): dead, numb,

Kwidi (*n*): worm, bacteria, virus,

Kwiny (*n*): dig, prod,

Kwinyo (daab) (*v*): mine,

Kwinyo (*v*): dig, mine, excavate,

Kwiri (*adj*): normal, conventional, gentle, sane,

Kwiri (*n*): poison

Kwiri (*n*): vote,

Kwiya piny (*adj*): ignorant,

Kwiya piny (*n*): ignorance,

Kwiya piny (*v*): ignorance,

Kwo (*adj*): alive, abiding, surviving, live, living,

Kwo (*v*): live, exist,

Kwok (*n*): sweat,

Kwok (tic, kero): work,

Kwon (*n*): food, mix cook water with flour,

Kwon ma miyo kero (ma gi noŋo ki kom ga macalo bel, liyata, gwana,) (*adj*): starchy,

Kwon ma miyo kero (*n*): cyborhydrates,

Kwon me doŋo (*adj*); protein,

Kwon me doŋo (*n*): protein,

Kwon me kero (*n*): carbohydrates,

Kwon me leŋo (*n*) vitamins,

Kwon me medo remo kacel ki me lweny ki two (*adj*): vitamins and mineral

Kwoŋ (*n*): pledge, vow,

Kwoŋo (*v*): swear, vow,

Kwoŋo yubo (*v*): invent, create,

Kwot (*adj*): lumpy,

Kwot (*adj*): whispered,

Kwot (*n*): indigestion,

Kwot (*n*): whisper,

Kwoto (*v*): whisper,

Kwoto kwot (v): confide,

Kwoyo (*v*): crochet,

Kwoyo (*v*): Knit, sew, stitch,

Kwriri ko (*adj*): aberrant, abnormal, unusual, deviant, anomalous, peculiar, irregular, atypical,

Kwriri ko (*adv*): abnormally,

L

La duny piny (*n*): brush, polish,

La dyere la dyere (*adj*): modest,

La gur (*n*): drive, hammer,

La rib lok (*n*): conjunction,

La tel lok (*n*): preposition,

La wac lok (*n*): phrase,

Laac (*adj*): vast, immense,

Labal (*adj*): criminal, offender,

Labal (*n*): sinner,

Labed naka (*adj*): everlasting, external,

Laber (*adj*): generous, kind, liberal, bighearted, openhanded, munificient, giving, charitable, altruistic, charming, gracious,

Labera (*n*): Liberia,

Labo (*n*): wrap,

Labok kom (*n*): bleach,

Labol (*adj*): exemplary, example,

Labol dog (*n, leg.*): applicant,

Labolo (*n*): banana,

Laboŋo (*prep.*): excluding, exclusive, minus, without,

Laboŋo a yela (*adj*): peaceful,

Laboŋo bal (*adj*): flawless, immaculate, spotless, perfect,

Laboŋo gen (*adv*): bleakly, forlornly, hopelessly, despondently, miserably, dejected, sorrowfully, sadly,

Laboŋo kec (*adv*): selflessly,

Laboŋo kit gi mo (*adv*): bleakly, forlornly, hopelessly, despondently, miserably, dejected, sorrowfully, sadly,

Laboŋo lewic (*adj*): unabashed,

Laboŋo lewic mo (*adv*): shamelessly,

Laboŋo lok (*adj*): deadpan, expressional, straight- faced, pokerfaced

Laboŋo nyero mo (*adj*): earnest, very serious,

Laboŋo nyero mo (*adv*): seriously,

Laboŋo ŋol (*adv*): continuously,

Laboŋo pak (*adj*): unsung,

Laboŋo tuko mo (*adj*): earnest, very serious,

Laboŋo tuko mo (*adv*): seriuosly,

Laboŋo tuti (*adv*): effortless,

Labuk ga (*n*): colour,

Labuk piny (tye, tibo tibo) (*n*): shade, hue,

Labuke (ki raŋi) (*n*): dye,

Labura (*adj*): bossy, domineering,

Labwolo (*n*): cheater, deceiver, tricker, swindler,

Labwomi (*adj*): murky, dishonest,

Labwomi (lacoo) (*adj*): knavish, cunning,

Labwomi (*n*): cheater,

Labwoti tic nyo kom (*adj*): outgoing,

Lac (*adj*): broad, huge, immense, wide,

Lac pa coo (*n*): semen,

Lacac (*adj*): naughty,

Lacan (*adj*): needy, poor, deprived, unfortunate, underpriviledge, broke, needy, destitute, poverty –stricken, destitute, impoverished,

Lacan (*n*): poor,

Lacaŋ mon (*n*): gyneacologist,

Lacaro (*adj*): irresponsible, careless, foolish,

Lacat (*n*): business man or woman, trader,

Lacat cuk (*n*): seller, trader, saler,

Lacat riŋo (*n*): butcher,

Lacen (*adv*): later,

Lacid ga (*n*): shade,

Laco (*n*): man,

Laco ma lacat (*n*): business man,

Lacoc (*n*): writer, author,

Lacuŋ (*n*): stop, brake,

Lacuŋo (*adj*): principle, responsible,

Lacuŋo dwar (*adj*): hero, legend,

Lacuŋo dwar (*n*): cover, insuarance,

Lacuŋo pi dul moni (*n, leg.*): representative proceedings,

Lacwak (*n*): advocate, supporter,

Lacwal kwena (*n*): press, journalist, presenter,

Lacwec (*n*): creator,

Lacwi (kwer, kwok) (*n*): pad,

Lacwi (*n*): straw,

Ladeyo (*adj*): smart, stylish, dapper, well-dressed, tidy, spruce, dashing, elegant,

Ladeyo (*adv*): fashionably,

Ladeyo (ruk) (*adj*): snappy, stylish,

Ladin waraga (*n*): stamp,

Ladiri (*adj*): productive, creative,

Ladit (me gaŋ kwan) (*n*): principle,

Ladit (*n*): superior, boss, manager, elder, chief, senior, director, supervisor, leader, executive, administrator, head,

Ladit (tic, lwak) (*adj*): responsible,

Ladit me gaŋ kwan (*n*): headmaster,

Ladit tic (*adj*): boss manager, director, supervisor,

Lador piny (*adj*): artistic,

Ladot (i kot) (*n, leg.*): plaintiff,

Ladot (*n*): reporter,

Ladwala (*n*): betrayer,

Ladwar (*n*): hunter,

Ladwar arabiya (*n*): driver,

Ladwar dege (*n*): pilot,

Ladwar meli (*n*): captain of the ship,

Ladyere (*adj*): average,

Ladyere (*n*): mean, average,

Lagam (*n*): answer,

Lageŋ det me bur (*n*): antiseptic,

Lageŋ nywal (*n*): contraceptive,

Lageto (*n*): architecture, builder,

Lagiŋi (*adj*): strict, subtle, stern,

Lagit (*adj*): ringed,

Lago gumi (*n*): boxer,

Lagoba (*adj*): dishonest, deceitful, untruthful, lying,

Lagoba (*n*): liar,

Lagony ic (*n*): laxative,

Lagony te coc (*n*): translator,

Lagony te lok (*n*): interpreter,

Lagur (*adj*): anchored,

Lagur (*n*): peg,

Lagwar (*n*): zebra,

Lagwe (*n*): lizard,

Lagwok (*n*): cover, insurance, protection, shelter,

Lagwok cene (*n*): treasurer,

Lagwok kuc (*n*): police, army,

Lajemo (*n*) rebel,

Lajog mucoro (*n*): tax collector,

Lajok (*n*): witch,

Lajwa (*n*): antelope,

Lajwa bau (*n*): carpenter,

Lak (*adj*): dental,

Lak (*n*): tooth,

Lak (*n*): wander,

Lakalatwe (*n*): star,

Lakec (*adj*): mean, stingy,

Lakec ko (*adj*): unselfish,

Lakec ko (*adv*): unselfish,

Lakee (*n*): niece,

Lakero (*adj*): powerful,

Laket (*n*): comb,

Laket cik (*n*): legislative,

Laket cik (*n, leg.*): Member of Parliament,

Lakica (*adj*): sympathetic, kind, warmhearted, affectionate, loving, kindhearted, compassionate, grace,

Lakica (*n*) grace, kindeness,

Lakido (*adj*): pattern,

Lakite (*adj*): dashing, stylish,

Lakite mo kenyo (*adv*): somehow,

Lakob (*n*): immigration,

Lakoda (*adj*): funny, daffy, lighthearted, playful,

Lakoda makwak (*adj*): hilarious,

Lakony (*n*): volunteer,

Lakony kor (*n, leg.*): agent,

Lakony tic ki lok (*n*): auxiliary verb,

Lakoŋo (*adj*): alcoholic,

Lakoŋo (*n*): alcoholic,

Lakricitayo (*n*): Christian,

Lakura (*n*): guard, watch,

Lakwan lim (*n*): accountant,

Lakwan lok aŋeya (*n*): presenter,

Lakwany - mac: (*adj*): negative,

Lakwaro (*n*): great grand daughter, great grand son,

Lakwat (*n*): shepherd,

Lakwe (*n*): brake,

Lakwe arem (*n*): painkiller,

Lakwe cwiny (*n*): counsellor,

Lakwele (*n*): prostitute,

Lakwena (*n*): disciple,

Lakwo (*adj*): corrupt (lit.) thief, crooked, dishonest, fraudulent,

Lakwo (*n*): thief,

Lakwo boŋo (*n*): tailor, dress maker,

Laleŋo (*adj*): dapper, neat, elegant, well-groomed, debonair

Laliŋ (*adj*): silent, quiet, mute, unspoken,

Laliŋ (*adv*): quietly,

Laliya (*n*): butter mixed with oil,

Laloji (ŋete ne moni piny doki tidi) (*adj*): lopsided,

Lalok aŋeya (*n*): press, journalist, reporter,

Lalok kwena (*n*): journalist, presenter,

Lalok lok aŋeya (*adj*): newscaster, anchored,

Lalonyo (*n*): rich,

Lalwok (ciŋ, Jami) (*n*): sink,

Lamak (*n*): frame, peg,

Lamake (*adj*): anchored,

Lamake (*n*): handle,

Lamaŋ (*adj*): mad, crazy, kooky,

Lamaro (*n*): cousin (lamaro),

Lami tam (*n*): adviser,

Lami tam (*n*): councellor,

Lamiŋ (*adj*): stupid, dimwitted, dopey, daffy,

Lamiŋ (*adv*): dopily,

Lamiŋ (*n*): dupe,

Lamok (*n*): peg,

Lamwol (*n*): pad,

Lamwon (*n*): glue,

Lamwon (*n*): paste,

Lamwony (*n*): soldier, army,

Lanede (*adj*): elegant, graceful, glamorous, lithe, skinny, svelte, slender, slim,

Lanen (*adj*): spotted, marked,

Lanen (*n*): monitor,

Lanen (*n*): label, mark, sign, notice, signal, trace,

Lanen cal (*n*): monitor,

Lanen me balo nyiŋ (*n*): brand,

Lanen mucero ikom (*n*): brand,

Lanyany (*adj*), abrasive, uncompromising,

Lanyany (*adj*): stubborn,

Lanyut (*adj*): evident, exemplary, example,

Lanyut (maber) (*adj*): quintessential,

Lanyut (*n*): lead, clue,

Lanywal dano (*n*): mid wife,

Laŋala (*n*): tease, joker,

Laŋet (*prep.*): beside,

Laŋol kop (*n*): judge,

Laŋol kop (*n, leg.*): crown prosecutor,

Laŋone (*adj*): anchored, attached,

Lapagano (*n*): pagan,

Lapidi (*n*): baby sitter, nurse,

Lapik (*n*): pump,

Lapim ic (*n*): ultrasound,

Lapim kom (*n*): x- ray

Lapiru (*n*): whirlwind, tornado, hurricane, cyclone,

Lapok lim (*n*): cashier,

Lapor (*n*): copy,

Lapor (*n*): quote, quotation,

Lapor (*n*): weiging scale,

Lapore pe (*adj*): eminent, outstanding, wonderful,

Lapoya (*adj*): crazy, mad, zany,

Lapuŋ (*n*): lock, seal,

Lapur (*n*): farmer, peasant,

Lapwony (*n*): coach, trainer, teacher,

Lapwony madit (*n*): professor,

Lapyem (*adj*): argumentative,

Lar (*n*): rescue,

Lar (*n*): rush,

Larac (*adj*): evil, impish, mischievous, wicked, villainous,

Lare ko (*adj*): indubitable, unquestionable,

Lareg (*n*): rib,

Larem (*adj*): friendly, warm, hospitable, welcoming,

Larem (*n*): friend, partner, companion, mate,

Larib wel (*n*): mathematics,

Lariŋo (*n*): athlete,

Laro (*adj*): hurry,

Laro (*v*): bargain,

Laro (*v*): rescue, save,

Laro kede (*v*): rush,

Laro lok (*n, leg.*): mediaition,

Laro lweny (*v*): swoop,

Laro wel (*n*): bargain,

Laro wot (*v*): pelt,

Larot piny (*n*): spy,

Larub (*n*): mix,

Laruk (*adj*): dashing, fashionable,

Latal (*n*): witch,

Latame (*adj*): clue,

Lataun (*adj*): dashing, urbane,

Latedo (*n*) cook, chef,

Latedo (*n*): chef,

Lateg (*n*): band-aids,

Latela (*adj*): leader,

Latela (*n*): head, leader,

Laten (*n*): frame,

Laten wic (*n*): pillow,

Later (*n*): transport,

Latic (ciŋ) (*n*): worker, labourer,

Latic ciŋ (*adj*): able, skilled, adept,

Latic me cik (*n*): lawyer,

Latic me cik (*n, leg.*): lawyer,

Latic me cik me kot madit (ma cuŋo pi lok moni i kot madit) (*n, leg.*): barrister, counsel,

Latima aranyi (*n*): criminal, offender,

Latin kwan (*n*): student,

Latir ga (*n*): editor,

Latiti lok aŋeya (*n*): press, journalist, reporter,

Latuc jiri (*n*): preacher,

Latuko odilo (*n*): footballer,

Latwe ne (*adj*): anchored, fasten,

Latwodo (*adj*): dishonest, lying, deceitful,

Latwodo (*n*): liar,

Latyen ariyo (*n*): second,

Latyer (*n*): star,

Laum (*n*): cover,

Laum waŋ (*n*): blind,

Lawaci kwena (*n*): anchor, newcaster,

Lawaci lok aŋeya (*n*): announcer,

Lawake (*adj*): lofty, proud, superior,

Lawaŋ ladit me gaŋ kwan (*n*): Deputy Head Master,

Lawaŋo too (*adv*): blindly,

Lawat (*adj*): welcoming, hospitable, generous,

Lawat puc (*adj*): feline,

Lawel (*adj*): digital,

Lawer (*n*): singer,

Lawi (coo, mon, bulu) (*n*): head,

Lawi lobo (*n*): president, prime minister, leader of a country or world,

Lawil (*n*): buyer,

Laworo (*adv*): yesterday,

Layab (*adj*): key,

Layak (*n*): robber,

Layeny (*n*): academic, researcher, investigator, scholar,

Layom cwiny (*adj*): cheerful, bright, happy, lively, kindhearted, cheery,

Layom cwiny (*adj*): generous, kind, liberal, bighearted, openhanded, munificient, giving, charitable,

Laywa yat (*n*): inhaler,

Laywe piny (*n*): cleaner, sweep,

Laywek (dano, ga) (*n*): transport,

Leb (*n*): discourse,

Leb (*n*): tongue,

Leb (*n*): voice, accent,

Leb munu me pa jo Pranc (*adj*): French,

Leb munu me Poland (*n*): polish,

Lebo (*n*): blister,

Lee (*n*): animal,

Lee gaŋ (*n*): pet,

Lega (*n*): prayer,

Lego (*v*): pray, meditate,

Leko (*v*): dream, fantasize, visualize, imagine, fancy daydream, envisage, hallucinate,

Lela (*n*): bicycle, cycle,

Lelek (*n*): dream,

Lem (*n*): cheek,

Lem ma oruŋ (calo ki nyero) (*adj*): dimple,

Lemo cwiny (*adj*): nauseated,

Lemo cwiny (*n*): travel sickness, nausea,

Leŋ (*adj*): beautiful, dashing, striking, attractive, handsome, good-looking, angelic, charming colour, form of grace, delight the eye and form of admiring, clean, glamorous, handsome, cute, pretty, gorgeous,

Leŋ (*adv*): beautifully, cutely,

Leŋ (boŋo) (*adj*): cool, fashionable,

Leŋ (coo) (*adj*): handsome,

Leŋ doki cer (*adj*): empty, bare,

Leŋ ki alur (*v*): inflate,

Leŋ ko (*adj*): ugly, unattractive, hideous, unsightly, repulsive, unsightly,

Leŋ ko (bot mon) (*adj*): plain,

Leŋ kom (*adj*): bonny,

Leŋ makwak (*adj*): lovely,

Leŋ pere yomo cwiny (*adj*): majestic,

Leŋe iye wa (*adj*): dependable, reliable,

Leŋo (I loko leb) (*n*): command,

Leŋo me kom (*n*): health,

Leŋo me tam (*n*): mental health,

Ler (*n*): muscle,

Ler yat (*n*): root,

Lero (*adj*): embarrassed,

Lewic (*adj*): shameful, disgraceful, reprehensible, dishonorable, discreditable, shocking, appaling, ashamed, abashed, embarrassed, mortified,

Lewic (*n*): shame, disgrace,

Lewic goyo ko (*adj*): shameless, brazen, bareface, unabashed, blatant, unashamed,

Lewic keken (*adj*): outrageous, disgraceful, shameful,

Leyo (*v*): adopt, succeed,

Leyo wic (*v*): criticize, disapprove of, condemn,

Leyo wic (*v*): pine, sulk,

Libe (*v*): pad,

Libealiba (*adj*): tiptoe

Libira me tuco dano (*n*): syringe,

Liceri (*n*): maize,

Lii (*adj*): direct, straight,

Lii (malo) (*adj*): upright,

Lii (*n*): straight, well,

Lilo (muŋ (*v*): bare,

Lilo dawn (*adj*): cooing,

Lilo dwan (*adj*): sniveling,

Lilo kom (*adj*): make-up,

Lim (*adj*): sugary, sweet,

Lim *(n)*: money,

Lim (*n*): visit, trip,

Lim dok (*adj*): persuasive, convincing,

Limo (*v*): trip,

Limo (*v*): visit,

Liŋ (*adj*): quiet, calm, silent,

Liŋ (*n*): quiet, silence,

Liŋ (piny) (*adj*): serene,

Liŋ manok (*n*): pause,

Liŋo (*v*): roll,

Liŋone koŋ manok (*adj*): muted,

Liro koko (*v*): sob,

Lit (*adj*): sick, ill, unwell,

Lit ka ogudo (kom) (*adj*): tender, sensitive, sore to the touch,

Lit kom (*adj*): queasy, unhealthy,

Lit kom (twero tic ko) (*adj*): unfit, unhealthy, in poor condition, ailing,

Liu (*adj*): piercing, loud,

Liu (dwan) (*adj*): shrill, sharp, loud, high –pitched, ,

Liwot (*n*): peer, friend, mate, partner,

Liwot pere pe (*adj*): unfriendly, abrasive, gruff, rude,

Liyata (*adj*): potato,

Liyata (*n*): potato,

Lobo (*n*): state, country, world, earth,

Lobol dog (*n, leg.*): applicants, appellants, respondents, defendants, etc., are generally called 'parties'

Lobolobo (boŋo) (*adj*): baggy,

Loc (*adj*): victory, ruling,

Loc (*n*): command, authority, control, power, defeat, reign, sway, win,

Loc ken (*adj*): independent, self-reliant,

Lodito (*adj*): elderly,

Logoro (*n*): crab,

Logule (*n*): elbow,

Logule adek (*adj*): triangle,

Logule adek (*adj*): triangular,

Lojo (*v*): barter, exchange, change,

Lok (*n*): exercise, problem,

Lok (*n*): argument, case, point,

Lok (*n*): contact, converse, talk, say,

Lok (*n*): word, utterance, statement, expression, speech, remark,

Lok (*v*): speak, talk,

Lok aŋeya (*n*): advertisement, announcement, program, agenda, release,

Lok aŋeya ma gi royo i magajin (waraga me lok aŋeya) (*n*): insert,

Lok atata (*v*): rave,

Lok gwoŋ gwoŋ (*v*): stammer, stutter,

Lok iye (*v*) stress,

Lok keket (*adj*): talkative, chatty,

Lok ki dog (*adj*): verbal,

Lok ma nwaŋ (*v*): falter,

Lok ma yeŋo waŋ dano (*n, leg.*): primacie facie case,

Lok macan (*adj*): plaintive,

Lok magi gonyo tyene woko (*adj*): paradoxical,

Lok maleŋ (*adj*): proficient, able,

Lok maleŋ (*v*): articulate,

Lok matiyo calo la wac lok i nyiŋ gi mo keken (*n*): pronoun,

Lok me ŋoc (*n, leg.*): statement of claim,

Lok me wi atii (*n, leg.*): case at first instance,

Lok oŋulebe (*v*): mumble,

Lok pa laŋol kop i ca me ŋolo kop (ma en aye pe kop ma gi ŋolo) (*n, leg.*): obiter dictum,

Loka (*n*): at the bank,

Loka (*prep.*): beyond,

Loka nam (*n*): over seas, beyond the river,

Loke (*adj*): rotating,

Loke (*n*): switch, change, shift, transfer,

Loke cokcok (*adj*): variable,

Loke ko (*adj*): stable, steady, perpetual, inflexible, uncompromising,,

Lokila (*n*): axe,

Loko (*n*): exchange, swap, turn,

Loko (*v*) reverse, swap, turn,

Loko kit (*adj*): disguised,

Loko kite aloka (*adj*): kaleidoscopic,

Loko kom (*adj*): disguised,

Loko lok (*v*): communicate, converse, convey,

Loko lok mogo madoŋo (*adj*): flowery, elaborate,

Loko loke (*v*): frame,

Loko otum woko ki doge (*adj*): deadpan, expressional, straight- faced, pokerfaced,

Loko tam wiye wiye (*v*): waver,

Loko wic yo kuca (*v*): face,

Loko wiye oyot (*adj*): fickle, changeable, indecisive, capricious, vacillating, unpredictable, erratic, picky, choosy,

Lokoro (*n*): throat,

Lokurakura (*adj*) critical, life- threatening,

Lokwano i dul ma apa (*adj*): decimal

Lolar lok (*n, leg.*): tribunal,

Loliro (*n*): bulb grass,

Lomi kwena (*n*): press, journalists,

Lony (*adj*) rich, fruitful, productive, successful, profitable, rewarding,

Lony ko (*adj*): disastrous, unsuccessful,

Lonyo (*adj*): richness, (n.) capital, assets, wealth, resource, funds, money, principal, investment, fortunate, priviledged, lucky, well-off, prosperous, rich,

Lonyo lonyo (*adv*): richly,

Lonyo magi noŋo ite ŋom (*n*): mine,

Loŋ (*n*): pair of trouser,

Loŋa aloŋa (*adj*): corrupt, dishonest, crooked, fraudulent,

Loŋe (*adj*): busy,

Loŋo (*adj*): blare, (*lit.*) high voice,

Loŋo (dek) (*v*): baste,

Loŋo (dwan) (*adj*): thunderous,

Loŋol kop (*n*): jury,

Loo (*v*): infuse,

Lor (*v*): roll,

Lor oyot oyot (*v*): swoop,

Lore (*prep.*): against, in opposition to,

Lori (*n*): lorry,

Lotim aranyi (*n*): gangster,

Lotino kwan (*n*): student,

Loyaŋ lee (*n*): butcher,

Loyo (*adj*) victorious, defeat, victory,

Loyo (*prep.*): than,

Loyo (*v*): command, control, rule, head, man, be incharge, govern, run, manage,

Loyo (*v*): defeat, beat,

Loyo (*v*): lose, be defeated,

Loyo (*v*): reign,

Loyo (*v*): subdue, control,

Loyo (*v*): win,

Loyo kit me (*v*): direct, manage,

Loyo kit me timo ne (*v*): dictate,

Loyo weŋ (*adj*): fantastic, excellent, terrific, superb, great, marvelous, fabulous, wonderful, tremendous, brilliant, eminent, outstanding, absolute, faboulos, grand, magnificent, mighty, optimal, powerful, prime, super, superior,

Loyo weŋ (*adv*): supreme, blissfully, mighty, tremendously, well, greatly,

Lubaŋa (*n*): God, god,

Lubaŋa kwedwa (*n*): God is with us, Emmanuel,

Lube kom twero (*adj*): official,

Lubo (*v*): follow, go after, track,

Lubo gina acoya ki cik me tela (*n, leg.*): practice notes and administrative notes,

Lubo gina acoyo (*n, leg.*): practice notes,

Ludoŋo (*adj*): elderly,

Ludoŋo (*n*): elders,

Lukoro (*n*): cancer,

Lukot (*n*): thunder,

Luloc ŋeyo (*adj*): formal,

Luloc pe ŋeyo (*adj*): informal,

Lum (*n*): grass,

Lumu (*adj*): raw (not ripe),

Lunyo (*v*): undress, strip,

Luŋga luŋga (*adj*): baggy,

Luŋo (*n*): tilt,

Luoc (*adj*): frosty,

Luro (*n*): spot, pimple,

Luru (*adj*): dusty,

Luru (*n*): dust,

Lwak (*n*): crowd,

Lwalalwala (*adj*): blond, dusty,

Lwar (*adj*): gray (hair), gray, grizzled,

Lwar ma orube ki matar ma menyo amenya (*adj*): silver,

Lweny (*adj*): assault, offensive, attacking,

Lweny (*n*): attack, violence, battle, fight, broil, brawl, fighting, fray,

Lweny (*v*): fight,

Lwenyo (*v*): attack, battle, broil, fight, brawl, row,

Lwet (*n*): finger,

Lwi (*adj*): sneaky,

Lwi (*n*): escape,

Lwi (*v*): escape,

Lwiny (*v*): dive, submerge, sink,

Lwite (*v*): sneak,

Lwiyo (*v*): whistle,

Lwoc (*n*): fog, snow,

Lwodo cwiny (*adj*): anxious, nervous, worried, concerned, uneasy, apprehensive, restless, fretful, jittery, murky, uptight, suspicious, wary, cautious, cagey, distrustful, circumspect, mistrustful, guarded,

Lwok (*n*): cleaning, shower, bathing, washing, wash,

Lwok (*v*): bath, bathe, clean, wash,

Lwok ki campu (*v*): shampoo,

Lwoka (*n*): okra,

Lwoke ko (moko) (*adj*): stained,

Lwoŋe (*n*): meeting, appointment,

Lwoŋo (kwon,) (*v*): order,

Lwoŋo (*n*): invite, invitation,

Lwoŋo (*v*): identify, name, call, invite,

Lwoŋo icim (*v*): telephone,

Lwoŋo maleŋ (*v*): enunciate, pronounce,

Lworo (*adj*): afraid, fearful,

Lworo (*adj*): anxiety,

Lworo (*adv*): coward,

Lworo (*n*): alarm, scare, fear, fright,

Lworo (*v*): fear,

Lworo muket (*n*): alarm, fear,

Lyec (*n*): elephant,

Lyel (*adj*): flickering, ablaze, inflame,

Lyel (*adj*): tomb, crpt, vault, burial place, burial chamber, mausoleum, sepulcher,

Lyel (*n*): funeral,

Lyelo (yer) (*v*): shave,

Lyero (*adj*): dangling, sagging,

Lyero (*n*): hanging, flaccid,

Lyero (*v*): dangle,

Lyet (*adj*): hot,

Lyet (*n*): heat,

Lyet bolo bolo (*adj*): warm,

Lyeto (ec) (*n*): toast,

Lyeto (ec) (*v*): toast,

Lyeto (*n*): fever,

Lyeto (*n*): heat, warmth,

Lyeto (*v*): heat,

Lyeto bolo bolo (*v*): warm,

Lyeto marac (*n*): glandular fever,

Lyeto me ceŋ (*n*): sunstroke,

Lyeto ne rac (*adj*): sweltering, very hot,

M

Ma (*prep.*): of,

Ma (*pron.*): that, which, who, whom, whose,

Ma cire ko (*adv*): unbearably,

Ma cuŋo i lok (*adv*): responsibly,

Ma cwiny pe iye (*adv*): tepidly,

Ma diri mo pe iye (*adv*): informally,

Ma dwoŋ (*adv*): Much,

Ma gene (*adv*): unfailingly,

Ma i gwoko waŋe agwoka (*adv*): strictly,

Ma i kit (calo pa dano) **weŋ** (*adv*): naturally,

Ma ipyemo ko (*adv*): genuinely,

Ma iye ocule (*adv*): solidly,

Ma ka tere pe (*adv*): vainly,

Ma ka tire pe (*adv*): vaguely,

Ma kakare (*adv*): truly,

Ma kala akala tye iye (*adv*): questionably,

Ma ki cwiny weŋ (*adv*): solemnly,

Ma kido pere pat (*adv*): quaintly,

Ma kite atir (*adv*): righteously,

Ma kite pat ko (*adv*): ordinarily,

Ma konye pe (*adv*): uselessly,

Ma konyo (*adv*): usefully,

Ma konyo kome wa (*adv*): responsibly,

Ma kore (tye, pe) (*adv*): subtly,

Ma kulu (*adv*): wholly,

Ma kweyo (*adv*): reassuringly,

Ma laboŋo bal (*adv*): perfectly,

Ma laboŋo lewic (*adv*): unabashedly,

Ma loke ko (*adv*): steady,

Ma loyo weŋ (*adv*): supremely

Ma loyo weŋ ne (*adv*): principally, above all,

Ma luloc pe ŋeyo (*adv*): informally,

Ma neni goba (*adv*): questionably,

Ma niaŋ ko (*adv*): superficially,

Ma noŋo ne tek (*adv*): rarely,

Ma nwaŋ (*adv*): solidly,

Ma nyaŋo ne yot (*adv*): plainly,

Ma nyaŋo ne yot (*adv*): simply, easily,

Ma ŋinyi ŋinyi ko (*adv*): superficially,

Ma ŋol ko (*adj*): steady, constant,

Ma obino atum gero ŋom (*adv*): zealously,

Ma obino ki apurukudaŋ (*adv*): zealously,

Ma ocobo (*adv*): successfully,

Ma ocouŋo gwir (*adv*): solidly,

Ma ocuŋo matek (*adv*): steady,

Ma ojul (*adv*): zealously,

Ma ojul (*adv*): zestily,

Ma oloko ki dog (*adv*): verbally,

Ma opore (*adv*): perfectly, properly, righteously,

Ma oroma aroma (*adv*): innocently,

Ma orwate (*adv*): properly,

Ma otamo iye matut (*adv*): thoughtfully,

Ma otere (*adv*): readily,

Ma otimo ki cwiny weŋ (*adv*): studiously,

Ma pe gi yubo ki iciŋ (*adv*): naturally,

Ma pe keto cwinye (*adv*): reluctantly,

Ma pe ki bal (*adv*) perfectly,

Ma pe ki ŋec (*adv*): skillfully,

Ma pe opore (*adv*): informally,

Ma pe tum (*adv*): evermore, perpetually,

Ma pire tek (*adv*): principally, chiefly, siginificantly, ultimately,

Ma pire tek (loyo weŋ) (*adv*): supremely,

Ma pire tek ko (*adv*): unnecessarily,

Ma piretek ne (*adv*): chiefly, mainly, mostly,

Ma pudi (*adv*): meanwhile,

Ma pwore wa (*adv*): impressively,

Ma rom (kede, ki en) (*adv*): worthily,

Ma rom rom (*adv*): commonly,

Ma romo (*adv*): sufficiently,

Ma rwate (*adv*): suitably,

Ma tamo dano (*adv*): thoughtfully,

Ma tidi keket (*adv*): slightly,

Ma tye atir (*adv*): primly,

Ma tye doki welo (*adv*): quaintly,

Ma tye ika ciŋ (*adv*): securely,

Ma tye Kakare (*adv*): properly, rightly,

Ma tye ki kero (*adv*): pontentially,

Ma tye ki miti me (*adv*): intently,

Ma winyo madiŋ (*adv*): terribly,

Ma wiye doŋo doŋo (*adj*): major,

Ma yomo cwiny makwak (*adv*): splendidly,

Maba (*adj*): default,

Maber (*adv*): suitably,

Maber (tito lok) (*adj*): vivid,

Maber ne (*adj*): important,

Mac (*adj*): fire, electric, light,

Mac (*n*): fire, electricity,

Mac (*n*): Mars,

Mac ma bedo purapura (*adj*): drab,

Macan (*adj*): miserable, woeful, unhappy, sorrowful, mournful, abject, wretched, dismal,

Macek (*adj*): brief, short, abrupt,

Macek cek (*adv*): briefly,

Macek keken (*adv*): shortly,

Macon (*adj*): previous, old-fashioned, quaint,

Maconi (*adv*): formerly,

Madako (*adj*): female,

Madit (*adj*): great, mammoth, vast,

Madit ne (*adv*): principally, mainly, largely,

Madwoŋ (*adj*): Many, massive,

Madwoŋ (*pron.*): many, several,

Madyak (*adj*): soggy,

Magi kobo (*n*): copy,

Magoba (*n*): return, profit, yield,

Makari (*n*): Mercury,

Makato ne (*adv*): acutely, acutely,

Make pa two (*n*): infection,

Maki (*n*): grab,

Mako (lok) (*n*): grasp,

Mako (lok) (*v*): grasp,

Mako (*n*): catch, arrest,

Mako (*n*): hold, grip, handle, grap,

Mako (rec,) (*v*): fish,

Mako (*v*): arrest, freeze, immobilize, get, catch, grab, clutch, hold, grasp,

Mako cal (*v*): film, shoot,

Mako cal ki ekcrei (macin) (*v*): x-ray,

Mako oyoto (*adj*): apt,

Mako tic (*v*): control, handle, manage, harness, control,

Mako wi dano (*n*): sulk,

Makwak (*adv*): dearly, very much, exceedingly, extremely, quite,

Malac (*adj*): wide, extensive, ample, enough, plenty,

Malaco (*adj*): male,

Malaga (*n*): spoon,

Malakwaŋ (*n*): hibiscus,

Male (*adj*): lacoo,

Maleŋ (leb) (*adv*): fluently,

Maleŋ (ngec i gi moni, I loko leb) (*n*): command,

Malo (*adj*): advanced, high, up,

Malo (*adv*): upward,

Malo (*prep.*): above, on top, up,

Man (*adj*): which,

Man (*n*): testicle,

Man (*pron.*): this,

Man (*pron.*): which,

Manga (*n*): mango,

Mani (*adj*): innocent, naive, shy,

Manok (*adv*): barely, scarcely, hardly, less, slightly,

Manok (*n*): minute,

Manok (*pron.*): few,

Manok nok (dire, cito, dok) (*adv*): gradually,

Maŋ (*adj*): mad,

Maŋ (*adv*): crazy, madly,

Maŋ (*n*): mad, crazy,

Map (*n*): map,

Mapat (*n*): converse,

Mape ber (*adj*): unfavourably,

Mape ŋol (*adv*): incessantly,

Mapudi (*adv*): before, while,

Mapudi (*conj.*): when, while, as,

Mapudi (*conj.*): before, rather than, otherwise,

Mapudi (*prep.*): before, ahead of,

Mapudi (*prep.*): by, not later than,

Mapudi (*prep.*): of, before,

Mar (*n*): love,

Mar (*v*): love,

Marac (*adj*): bad, deadly, fatal, serious, grave, critical, severe, crucial, mortal, somber, woeful,

Marac (*adj*): worse,

Marac (*adv*): badly,

Marac keket (*adv*): seriously, solemnly,

Marac makwak (*adv*): terribly,

Mare (*adj*): likeable, lovable,

Marmar (*adj*): pink,

Maro (*adj*): fond, loving, love,

Maro (*v*): favour, prefer, love,

Maro bedo ki dano (*adj*): sociable,

Maro dano (*adj*): generous, kind, liberal, bighearted, openhanded, munificient, giving, charitable, gregarious, sociable,

Maro loyo weŋ (*v*): dote,

Maro peny (*adv*): inquisitive,

Marom aroma (*adv*): evenly,

Mat (*adj*): drink,

Mat (*n*): brew, drink,

Matek (*adj*): concrete (lit) strong, abrasive, harsh, stiff,

Matek (*adj*): intense, vigorous, rigorous, hard, severe,

Matek (*adv*): fast, firmly, sternly, vigorously,

Matidi ki liŋ diu (*adj*): miniature,

Mato (*v*): drink, smoke,

Mato koŋo makwak (*v*): sodden,

Matut (*adv*): deeply,

Matwal (la) (*adv*): forever,

Mayaŋ (*adv*): formerly,

Mayot (*adj*): plain,

Mayot (*adv*): lightly,

Me (*prep.*): of,

Me a deke (*adj*): third,

Me acel (*adj*): first,

Me ariyo (*adj*): second,

Me awora (*adj*): venerated, respected, acclaimed, adored, highly thought of, recognized,

Me bedo gaŋ (boŋo) (*adj*): informal (cloths),

Me cwiny (*adv*): spiritually,

Me diŋo (yat) (*adv*): sedately,

Me gaŋ (*adj*) tame, domestic,

Me gaŋ (dano) (*adj*): homely,

Me i kare eni (Jami, ga) (*adj*): modern,

Me lobo (*adj*): wordly, mortal, earthly,

Me lweny (muduku) (*adj*): offensive,

Me nono (*adj*): free,

Me nono (*adv*): freely,

Me polo (*adj*): heavenly,

Me te nino ni (*adv*): currently,

Me teko (*adj*): strenuous, vigorous,

Me wel (*adj*): precious,

Meda ameda (*adj*): perpetual,

Mede (*n*): climb, increase, rise,

Mede (*v*): continue, carry on, develop, expand, keep, hang on, remain, continue,

Mede ameda (*adv*): evermore, increasingly,

Mede anyim (*adj*): advanced,

Mede ki (*v*): proceed, go on,

Medi iye (*prep.*): plus,

Medi kom eni (*adv*): furthermore,

Medo (*v*): add, add up, extend, increase,

Medo adaa (*adj*): elaborate,

Medo kado (i lok) (*n*): twist,

Medo kero (*n*): lift,

Medo lok (*adj*): aggravate, worsen, exacerbate, make worse, intensify,

Medo ŋec (*adj*): elaborate,

Medo remo (*n*): transfusion,

Medo rwom (*v*): encourage, promote,

Mego (*n*): mother, mum,

Meja (*n*): table,

Meny (*adj*): flash,

Menyo (*adj*): shiny, glossy, gleaming, sparkly, glittery, polished, shimmering, glistening, burnished, radiant, luminous, lustrous, dazzling,

Menyo (*n*): shining,

Menyo (*v*): beam, flash, light,

Menyo pilak (*n*): flash,

Mic (*adj*): gifted, brilliant, talented, (*lit.*) gift, able,

Mic (*n*): present, gift, bid, offer, proposal, supply, provision,

Mic pere (*adj*): gifted,

Mii (*adj*): close, closed,

Milion (*n*): million,

Min lwet ciŋ (*n*): thumb,

Min lwet tyelo (*n*): toe,

Mine (*n*): twist,

Mino (*n*): twist,

Minya (*adj*): delirious,

Miŋ (*adj*): foolish, idiot, silly,

Miŋo (*adj*): silly, stupid, ridiculous, childish, insane, idiotic,

Mit (*adj*): delicious, delightful, delectable, tasty, yummy,

Mit (ka ibilo) (*adj*): palatable, pleasant to taste,

Mit (*n*): delicious, good, savour,

Mit ko (*adj*): unpleasant,

Mit ko makwak (*adj*): obnoxious, noxious,

Mit kom (*adj*): animated, lively, vigorously, sparkling, active, vivacious, dynamic, bubbly, spirited, jaunty, jolly, nimble, spirited, vibrant, vital,

Mit kom (*adv*): actively,

Mit kom me kwan (*adj*): studious,

Mite (*adj*): admirable, required,

Mite (*n*): demand, requirement, need, essential,

Mite (*n*): taste,

Miti (*adj*): affectionate, passionate, zealous,

Miti (mar, rwate, timo gin moni) (*adj*): passionate,

Miti (me timo gi moni) (*n*): aim, goal,

Miti (*n*): want, need, demand, drive, urge, push, interest, passion, wish, desire,

Miti (pi gin moni) (*adj*): passion,

Miti me kom (*adj*): passion,

Miti me kom (*n*): heat, passion,

Miti mekom marac (*adj*): passion,

Miti pere peke iye (*adj*): do not want,

Mito (*adj*): admired,

Mito (*v*): demand, require, expect, need, like, want,

Mito (wel) (*v*): stipulate, demand,

Mito ga pa dano (*v*): covet,

Mito ko (*adj*): unwilling, reluctance,

Mito mwony (*adj*): warlike,

Mito ŋec (*adj*): demanding,

Mito tim miŋo ko (*adj*): staid, unadventurus, conservative,

Mito too ki yom cwiny (*adj*): delirious, ecstatic, euphoric,

Miya (*n*): hundred,

Miya abic (*n*): five hundred,

Miya abicel (*n*): six hundred,

Miya abiro (*n*): seven hundred,

Miya aboŋwen (*n*): nine hundred,

Miya aboro (*n*): eight hundred,

Miya acel (*n*): one hundred,

Miya adek (*n*): three hundred,

Miya aŋwen (*n*): four hundred,

Miya ariyo (*n*): two hundred,

Miyo (*adj*): giving,

Miyo (kwon) (*v*): serve,

Miyo (*v*): give, provide, hand, lend, present, give to, impart,

Miyo (*v*): offer, present, supply, provide,

Miyo cac (*adj*): embarrassed,

Miyo cik (*n*): command, directive,

Miyo cik (*v*): encode, program, instruct, command, order,

65

Miyo den (*v*): loan,

Miyo ga (*v*): produce, present something,

Miyo gin moni ki woro (*n*): treat,

Miyo gum (*v*): bless,

Miyo kare (winy) (*n*): say, voice,

Miyo kom (*adj*): abiding, steadfast,(*lit.*) giving oneself,

Miyo kom (*adj*): devoted, dutiful, obedient, devoted, faithful, oblinging, submissive, submit, obey, volunteer, (*lit.*) giving one self, voluntary,

Miyo kom (ka timo gi mo makelo can) (*v*): venture,

Miyo kom (*v*): volunteer,

Miyo lewic (*v*): disappoint, embarrass,

Miyo mic (ma pire tek) (*v*): bestow,

Miyo ŋec (*n*): caution,

Miyo tam (ki cwiny weŋ) (*v*): urge,

Miyo tam (*n*): trace, suggestion,

Miyo tam (*v*): advise, suggest, hint,

Miyo tam ni gi mo marac bitime (*adj*): ominous,

Miyo tic ma onoŋo pe omii (bot ŋatmo) (*adj*): lumbering,

Miyo twero (*adj*): authorize

Miyo twero (*v*): command, order, invest, endow, permit, authorize, license,

Mizan (*n*): weiging scale,

Mo (*pron.*): some,

Mo keken (*adj*): any, every,

Mo keken (*adv*): every,

Mo keken (*pron.*): any, whichever,

Mocura (*n*): tap,

Moko (*adj*): fixed,

Moko (*n*): fix, stick,

Moko (*n*): flour,

Moko (*n*): jam, freeze, halt,

Moko (*v*): attach, fasten,

Moko (*v*): Jam,

Moko (*v*): set, establish, settle, stay,

Moko (*v*): trap,

Moko amoka (*n*): freeze,

Moko icik (Acholi) (*adj*): conventional, conservative

Moko ijwen (*adj*): loyal, obedient,

Moko ikom (*adj*): stained,

Moko iye kiŋ kiŋ (*adj*): persistent,

Mol (*v*): flow,

Mono (*adj*): breakable, fragile, delicate, brittle, frail,

Moo (*n*): grease,

Moo kic (*n*): honey,

Moo maŋwece kur (*adj*): perfumed,

Moomoo (*adj*): cream,

Moro (*adj*): nutritious,

Moro dwan (*adj*): snarling, growl, roar,

Moro dwan (*v*): roar, thunder,

Moro koko (*v*): bawl,

Moro lweny (*n*): storm,

Moro waŋ (*n*): gaze,

Moro waŋ (*v*): gaze,

Mot (*adj*) calm, (*lit.*) peacefully,

Mot (*adj*): slow,

Mot (*adj*): sorry,

Mot (*n*): greeting, shaking hand,

Mot kede (*adj*): sorry (condolence),

Mot kede (*adj*): sorry,

Motara ma tye calo aluu –yamo (*adj*): gaseous,

Motmot (*adv*): slowly

Moto (*v*): acknowledge, greet, hail,

Moto mot (*n*): wave,

Moto mot (*v*): wave,

Mucer (*n*): saw,

Muculo (*adj*): chubby, plumped, thick

Mudolo adola (*n*): roll,

Mugu (*pron.*): these,

Muk (*adj*): flaky,

Mukene (*adj*): another, one more, an extra, any more, an alternative, an additional, any, next, other, second, next, subsequent, following, succeeding, some,

Mukene (*adv*): extra, more, next, subsequently,

Mukene doki to (*adv*): moreover,

Mukora (*adj*): crooked,

Mukwoŋo (*adj*): aboriginal, original,

Mul (*n*): pat, touch, trace,

Mulo (*v*): crawl,

Mulo (*v*): pat, touch,

Mulony (*adj*): wealthy, rich, well-off, affluent, prosperous,

Muŋ (*adj*): private, secret, mysterious,

Muŋado otwo ne (*adj*): crisp,

Muŋe ko (*adj*): honest, truthful, sincere, frank, candid,

Muromo (*adj*): abundant,

Mutakari (*n*): car,

Mutere (*n*): (dry raisin) potato sliced and dried,

Mutere (*n*): chip,

Muto (*v*) milk, exploit,

Muyai (*n*): prostitute,

Muyembe (*n*): mango,

Muziŋa (*n*): bomb,

Mwaka (*n*): year,

Mwoc (muduku) (*n*): crack,

Mwoc (*n*): pop, explosion, bang,

Mwoc (*v*): explode, pop,

Mwodo (*n*): star grass,

Mwol (*adj*): humble, gentle, meek, courteous, polite, well-mannered (*lit*) humble, shy, introverted, withdrawn, reserved, timid, tender,

Mwol (*adj*): poor, humble,

Mwol (*n*): flow, current,

Mwol (*n*): trickle,

Mwol (*v*): gush, overflow,

Mwol (*v*): trickle,

Mwole (*v*): submit,

Mwolo (*v*): tame,

Mwon (*adj*): attached, (*lit*) closed, filled

Mwon (*n*): stick,

Mwono (*v*): attach, glue, build, pad,

Mwono (*v*): paste, stick,

Mwono bur (*n*): dressing,

Mwony (*n*): battle, wage war,

Mwony (*v*): drown,

Mwony ki pii (*v*): flood,

Mwonya (*adj*): attractive, beautiful, charming, delectable, glamorous, stunning, dashing, debonair, striking, suave, dazzling, alluring,

Mwonya (dako) (*adj*): handsome,

Mwonyo (*v*): battle, fight, wage war,

Myel (*n*): hop, dance,

Myel (*v*): dance,

Myel kom (*n*): shiver, alarm,

Myelo kom (*adj*): scared, frightened, terrified, timid,
petrified, gruesome, ghastly, horrible, horrific, horrid,
shocking, dreadful, frightening, macabre, repugnant,
hideous, panicky, alarm, alarming, creepy, scary, horrible,

Myelo kom (v): alarm, frightened, terrify, frighten, scare,

N

Naka naka (*adv*): always,

Nam (*n*): lake, river (big), sea, ocean

Naŋo (*v*): lick,

Nebi (*n*): prophet,

Nek (*n*): murder,

Neko (*v*): kill, slay, murder,

Neko cene (cat) (*n*): venture,

Neko lee (*v*): butcher,

Neko waŋ (*v*): blind,

Nekone koŋ manok (*adj*): muted,

Nen (*adj*): visual,

Nen (*n*): look, gaze, watch,

Nen (*n*): visit, appointment,

Nen (*v*): appear,

Nen (*v*): look, see, notice, observe,

Nen calo ok (*prep.*): around, approximately,

Nen cok cok (*adj*): periodic,

Nen ko (*adj*): invisible,

Nen koŋ (*v*): comment, observe, spot,

Nen ni (*adv*): superficially,

Neni (*adj*): seem,

Neni (*adv*): likely, possibly,

Neni calo (*adv*): probably,

Neni lagoba (*adj*): questionable,

Neni time ko (*adj*): improbable,

Neno (*n*): look, appearance,

Neno (*n*): sight,

Neno (*n*): visit, stay,

Neno (*pre*: gine) (*adv*): appreciably,

Neno (*v*): control, monitor,

Neno (*v*): saw,

Neno (*v*): sound, seem,

Neno can (*adj*): miserable,

Neno doki dano makwiri (*adj*): dapper, debonair

Neno marac (*adj*): awkward, hideous, klutzy,

Neno marac ki boro pere ne doki colcol (*adj*): lanky,

Neno pat (*adj*): oddball,

Neno purapura (*adj*): fuzzy,

Neno pworopworo (*adj*): murky,

Neno rac (*adj*): unsightly,

Ner (*adj*): wither,

Nero (*n*): uncle (mother side),

Nga (*pron.*): who,

Ngabe pa cwiny (*adj*): anxiety,

Ngabo cwiny (*adj*): tense, anxious, nervous,

Ngade (*adj*): flaky, peeling, detaching, coming off,

Ngado (*v*): peel,

Ngado (*v*): peel, slice,

Ngala (*adj*): sardonic, scornful, mocking, sarcastic, ironic, satirical,

Ngala (*n*): attack, criticism,

Ngala (*n*): jeer, scoff, mock,

Ngala ŋala (*adj*): wry, ironic, cynical, sardonic,

Ngalo (*v*): jeer, scoff, mock, tease,

Ngamo (*adj*): yawning,

Ngamo (dogolo nyo waŋ ot) (*adj or adv*): ajar,

Ngamo (*v*): yawn,

Ngat ma ngere (*n*) celebrity, famous,

Ngat ma ocuŋo pire kene i kot (*n, leg.*): self represented litigant,

Ngat ma odule ka winyo lok i kot (*n, leg.*): litigant,

Ngat ma okwoŋo bolo doge i kot (*n, leg.*): appellant,

Ngat ma tye i dul pa lo tic me cik (*n*): bar,

Ngat malok ki lotto (*adj*): mediums,

Ngat mo (*pron.*): someone,

Ngat mo …pe (*pron.*): nobody, no one,

Ngat mo keken (*pron.*): anybody, anyone,

Ngat mo keken (*pron.*): each, everyone,

Ngat mo keken (*pron.*): whoever, whomever,

Ngat mo nyo dul pa dano mo magi tye ki twero (*adj*): official,

Ngat mudoto i kot (*n, leg.*): respondents,

Ngat mukelo i kot (ma oŋolo kop i wiye) (*n, leg.*): defendant,

Nge buk (*n*): cover,

Ngec (*adj*): aware, detailed, information, experienced, witty, knowledge,

Ngec (*adj*): confident, bouncy,

Ngec (me tic moni) (*n*): trade, skill,

Ngec (*n*): experience,

Ngec (*n*): back,

Ngec (*n*): drive, campaign,

Ngec (*n*): notice, warning,

Ngec (paŋo odilo) (*n*): control,

Ngec kit me nyut (*adj*): descriptive,

Ngec me dolo ciŋ ki tyelo i tuko (*adj*): acrobatic,

Ngec me tela (*n, leg.*): administrative notices,

Ngec me timo gin moni (*adj*): adept,

Ngene (*n*): stain,

Ngene (*v*): stain,

Ngeno cwiny (*adj*): irritable, rude,

Ngeno lok (*adj*): offensive, rude, abusive, wooden,

Ngeno lok (*n*): retort,

Ngeno lok (*v*): grate, say something in a harsh voice, retort,

Ngeŋ (*adj*): puzzle,

Ngeŋ (*n*): stunt,

Ngeŋ (*v*): stunt,

Ngere (*adj*): darling (media), flamboyant,

Ngere (*adj*): determined,

Ngere (*adj*): esteemed, familiar, notable,

Ngere ko (*adj*): unknown,

Nget cwiny (*n*): regret, disappointment,

Ngete (*adj*): partial,

Ngete (*n*): share, part, slice,

Ngete tum cel (*adj*): unilateral,

Ngeto cwiny (*adj*): irritation, annoyance, incense, exasperate, filthy, indecent, offensive, aggravate, annoy, irritate, provoke, make angry, frustrate, agitate, disgusting, enraged, irritating, loathsome, nasty, outrageous, shocking, pesky, annoying, shocked, offended, shocking, unacceptable,

Ngeto cwiny (*adj*): upset,

Ngeto cwiny (*v*): annoy, grate, irritate, inflame, offend, ride,

Ngeto cwiny (*v*): fume,

Ngeye (*n*): cover, covering,

Ngeyo (*adj*): known,

Ngeyo (*adj*): knowing,

Ngeyo (*v*) identify, spot, recognize, acknowledge,

Ngeyo (*v*): know, be acquainted with, identify, understand, experience,

Ngeyo (*v*): realize, recognize, sense,

Ngeyo kit me lok (*adv*): eloquent,

Ngeyo kite tek (loko wiye ki tam pere ca mo keken) (*adj*): fickle, changeable, indecisive, capricious, vacillating, unpredictable, erratic, picky, choosy,

Ngeyo ko (*v*): wonder,

Ngeyo kome (*adj*): conscious,

Ngeyo kome ko (*adj*): unconscious, dead, insensitive

Ngeyo muŋ ne tek (*adj*): shadowy,

Ngic (*adj*): cold, arctic, cool, damp, moist,

Ngic (*n*): bite, coldness, cold,

Ngic (*n*): check, inspection,

Ngic doki titii (*adj*): chilly

Ngic makwak (*adj*): frigid,

Ngic titi (*adj*): piercing, cold,

Ngico (ka luoc oumo piny) (*adj*): frosty,

Ngico (*n*): cold,

Ngido (*n*): drizzling,

Ngii (*v*): examine, look at, explore, inspect, examine, observe,

Nginaŋina (*adv*): awkwardly,

Ngine (yer) (*adj*): frizzy,

Ngino gumi (*v*): box,

Nginye (arem, cwer cwiny) (*adj*): writhing,

Nginye ki arem (*v*): writhe,

Nginye woko (*adj*): insubstantial,

Nginyi ŋinyi ko (*adj*): superficial,

Ngire (*adj*): dare,

Ngit (*n*): brain,

Ngit wiye pe (*adj*): thoughtless,

Ngiyo (*adj*): quaint,

Ngiyo atir (tic pa kot me yenyo atir) (*n, leg.*): determination of fact,

Ngiyo iye (*adj*): critical, analytic, logical, investigative,

Ngiyo iye (*v*): analyze,

Ngiyo iye (*v*): assess,

Ngiyo iye (*v*): balance, assess,

Ngiyo ŋoc (ikin jo mu doto gin) (*n, leg.*): cross claim,

Ngo (*pron.*): what,

Ngo (*v*): melt, melted, thaw, melt,

Ngoc (calo cwinyi cwer nyo itye imar nyo itamo gi mukato aŋec) (*adj*): sentimental,

Ngoc (*n*): claim, assertion,

Ngok (*n*): vomit,

Ngol (*adj*): lame,

Ngol (*n*): cut,

Ngol (*n*): lame,

Ngol (*v*): cut, slash,

Ngol aŋola (*adj*): jumpy,

Ngol ko (*adj*): constant, steady, stable, even, invariable, unvarying, regular, continuous, endless, recurring, frequent, recurrent, incessant, relentless, continual, unremitting, persistent, perpetual, unbroken, unceasing,

Ngole (*v*): interfere,

Ngole iye (*v*): interrupt,

Ngolo (*v*): cross, intersect, transverse, cut,

Ngolo cul (*n, leg.*): party and party cost,

Ngolo dog (*v*): interject,

Ngolo kop (*n, leg.*): judgment,

Ngolo kop (*v*): judge,

Ngom (*adj*): dusty,

Ngom (*n*): earth, land,

Ngom ma twolo (n, leg.): terra nullius,

Ngono (*v*): grab, clutch,

Ngoo doki pii (*adj*): waterlogged,

Ngoyo (*v*): allege,

Ngoyo (*v*): pretend,

Ngoyo aŋoya ko (ŋec) (*adj*): first hand,

Ngoyo kit me timo ga (*v*): dictate,

Ngoyo kom (*v*): pretend,

Ngoyo laa (*adj*): interesting, appealing,

Nguko (*adj*): untimely,

Nguko (*n*): gurgle,

Nguko (*v*): gurgle,

Ngulo lok (*n*): comment, criticism, remark,

Ngunde (*adj*): cynical, resent,

Ngunde (*n*): protest,

Ngundo (*n*): cut, reduction,

Ngundo macek (*adj*): snappy, interesting to the point,

Ngundo yip lee (*v*): dock

Nguno (ilok)(*adj*): elliptical,

Ngur (*adj*): grouchy, grumpy, complaining,

Ngur (gwok) (*adj*): growling,

Nguro (*adj*): grumpy, complaining,

Nguro (gwok) (*n*): growl, snarl,

Nguro (gwok) (*v*): growl,

Nguro (koko pa kic) (*adj*): humming,

Nguro (*n*): grumble, complaint, groan, drone, snarl, whine,

Nguro (riyo) (*v*): besiege,

Nguro (*v*): buzz,

Nguro (*v*): drone,

Nguro (*v*): grumble, complain, groan,

Nguro (*v*): snarl,

Nguro (*v*): stutter, sputter,

Nguro (*v*): whine,

Nguro dwane matek (*v*): hoot,

Ngut (*adj*): remorseful, regretful, sorry, repentant, penitent, contrite, apologetic, rueful,

Ngut (*n*): regret, remorse,

Ngut (*n*): neck,

Ngut (*v*): confess, own, regret,

Ngut ciŋ (*n*): wrist,

Ngwate (*adj*): proud,

Ngwec (lela, arabia) (*n*): ride,

Ngwec (*n*): run, trot,

Ngwec (*n*): smell, odour, reek, stink,

Ngwece kur (*adj*): aromatic,

Ngwece ne otiŋo piny (*adj*): pungent,

Ngweco (*v*): jog,

Ngweko (cal, coc,) (*n*): print, pattern,

Ngweko kom ki coko ga mogo ikom calo akanya ŋo (imyel) (*adj*): frillly,

Ngweyo (ga makur ki ma olulo piny) (*adj*): scented,

Ngweyo (ni gimo time) (*adj*): scented,

Ngwido (*adj*): analyse, breakdown,

Ngwido (*v*): chip, chop, grate, make into small,

Ngwido lok (*v*): nag,

Ngwiny (*n*): grasp,

Ngwinye pa ic (*n*): gastroenteritis,

Ngwinyo (*n*): pinch,

Ngwinyo (*v*): grip, grasp, pinch,

Ngwinyo (*v*): pinch,

Ni rii kec (*n*): fast,

Nia (*conj.*): that,

Niaŋ (*adj*): thoughtful,

Niaŋ (*n*): level, intensity,

Niaŋ (*n*): understanding,

Niaŋ ko (*adj***)**: superficial,

Nining (*adv*): how,

Nino (*n*): day,

Nino (*n*): sleep,

Nino (*v*): sleep,

Nino ducu (*adj*): daily, everyday,

Nino ki nino (*adj*): daily, day by day, day after day, each day

Nino mo keken (*adj*): daily, each day,

Nino ne okato (*adj*): overdue,

Nino nino (*adj*): sleepy, drowsy,

Nino weŋ (*adj*): daily, on a daily basis,

Nio (*conj.*): till, unless, except, until,

Nio (*prep.*): until,

Nio wa kany (*adv*): considerably, to a great extent, hitherto,

Niyee (*adj*): believe, acceptance, obedient,

Niyee (ikin locat) (*n*) deals,

Niyee (*n*): acclaim, approval,

Niyee (*n*): consent,

Niyee (*n*): deal, contract, order,

Niyee (*n*): guarantee, assuarance,

Nok (*adj*): few, small number, the minority, not many, hardly any, meager, measly, scarce, in short supply, limited, inadequate, scant, insufiicient, sparse, meager,

Nok (*n*): finitely, limited,

Nok ki (*prep.*): below, less than,

Nok me dul pa remo makwar (*n*): anaemia,

Nono (*adj*): bare, (*lit.*) without anything, nothing,

Noŋ *(n*): finding, discovery,

Noŋ (*n*): contact,

Noŋ (*n*): mark, score,

Noŋ (penyo ka ka gina acoyo me pyem ni weŋ tye ikin jo ma tye i pyem) (*n, leg.*): discovery,

Noŋe (*n*): meeting, encounter,

Noŋo (*n*): find, discovery,

Noŋo (*v*): earn, make, found, have, obtain, get, identify, discover, find, draw, make, catch, contract, receive,

Noŋo (*v*): land, acquire,

Noŋo (*v*): win,

Noŋo can (*v*): suffer,

Noŋo ne tek (*adj*): rare,

Note (*v*): kiss,

Noto (*n*): kiss,

Nucu (*adj*): half,

Nukta (*adj*): dot, point, spotted, dotted,

Nur (*n*): burden, lumber,

Nur (*n*): snooze,

Nur (*n*): stress,

Nur (*v*): burden, lumber,

Nur (*v*): nod, doze,

Nur ki cwer cwiny (*adj*): depressed,

Nuro (nino,) (*adj*): dopey,

Nuro (*v*): snooze,

Nwaŋ (*adj*): solid, wiry,

Nweyo kom (*adj*): submissive,

Nweyo kom (*v*): relax,

Nwoc (*adj*): repeated,

Nwore (*adj*): recurring, frequent, recurrent, incessant, relentless, continual, unremitting, persistent, perpetual, unbroken, unceasing,

Nwoyo (*v*): reiterate, repeat,

Nwoyo a nwoya (*adv*): repeatedly,

Nwoyo bako dog (ŋolo cik) (*n, leg.*): reappeal,

Nwoyo coc (*v*): notice, write review of something,

Nya (*n*): copy, reproduction, print, reproduce,

Nya (*v*): breed, produce, generate, increase, multiply, expand, yield something,

Nyak (*v*): yield, bear, produce,

Nyako (*n*): girl,

Nyale i kom (*v*): befriend,

Nyalo (*adj*): attractive, persuade, convince,

Nyalo (*v*): attract, cajole, coax, persuade, encourage,

Nyalo dano (*adj*) quaint, appealing, dazzling, alluring,

Nyamo (*n*): chew,

Nyamo (*v*): gnaw, chew, chomp,

Nyamo lok i kom gin moni (*n*): discourse,

Nyany (*adv*): arrogantly,

Nyanya (*adj*): tomato,

Nyanya (*n*): tomato,

Nyaŋ (*adj*): understand, comprehend, know, grasp, value, realize, recognize, empathize, educated, sophisticated, cultured, courteous, considerate, cultivated, educated, urbane, silicitious,

Nyaŋ (*n*): crocodile,

Nyaŋ (*n*): sense, get, understand,

Nyaŋ Koŋ (*v*): confirm,

Nyaŋ kwe (*adj*): dull,

Nyaŋ oyoto (*adj*): agile, understand,

Nyaŋ tere (*adj*): critical, analytic, logical, investigative,

Nyaŋo (*adj*): elaborate, enlightened,

Nyaŋo adaa me lok ki bot lacaden (*v*): cross-examine,

Nyaŋo dano ko (*adj*), flimsy, unconvincing, inadequate,

Nyaŋo kate lok (*n*): research, investigation,

Nyaŋo katere (*v*): examine, investigate, research,

Nyaŋo ne tek (*adj*): complex, (*lit.*) difficult to understand, complicated, mysterious,

Nyaŋo ne yot (*adj*): plain, simple,

Nyap kom (*adj*): lazy, fumble,

Nyar (*n*): daughter,

Nyar (*n*): puberty,

Nyate (*adj*): proud, arrogant, narcissistic, vainglorious, self-important, bigheaded, awkward, vain, conceited,

Nyayo (*adj*): calculating,

Nyayo lok (*adj*): aggravate, worsen, exacerbate, make worse, intensify,

Nyeko (*adj*): jealous,

Nyeko (*n*): jealousy,

Nyeko (*n*): jealousy, envy,

Nyen (*adj*): new,

Nyen iye pudi (*adj*): inexperienced,

Nyene (ki woo) (*v*): hail, attract attention,

Nyene (*v*): exhort, upstage,

Nyero (*n*): laugh,

Nyero (*v*): laugh,

Nyero kadi ki lwoŋo (*adj*): hysterical,

Nyero ko (*adj*): serious,

Nyeto (*v*): sputter,

Nyig lok (*n*): point, detail,

Nyik kic (*n*): bee,

Nyim (*n*): sesame,

Nyiŋ (*n*): name, reputation,

Nyiŋ gi mo keken (*n*): noun,

Nyiŋe obale woko (*adj*): infamous,

Nyo (*conj.*): or, otherwise,

Nyo...pe (*conj.*): neither ...nor,

Nyobo (*adj*): mixed,

Nyobo (*v*): mix,

Nyol (*n*): hammer,

Nyom (*adj*): married,

Nyomo (*v*): marry,

Nyomo nyom (*v*): wed,

Nyondo (*n*): hammer,

Nyono (katyene) (*v*): step,

Nyono (lela,) (*v*): pedal,

Nyono (*v*): stamp, trample,

Nyono lela (*n*): ride,

Nyono lela (*v*): cycle, ride,

Nyonyo (*n*): iron,

Nyonyo me tucu pii (*n*): drill,

Nyonyo me tweyo ga (*n*): screw,

Nyoŋ (*n*): crush,

Nyoŋo (ot) (*v*): shade,

Nyoŋo (*v*): crush,

Nyoŋo (*v*): squeeze,

Nyote pa kom (*adj*): bored, jaded, world –weary, tired, worn –out, fed- up,

Nyote pa kom (*adj*): stress,

Nyugi (*n*): lice,

Nyune (*adj*): dense,

Nyunye pa gudu (*n*): jam,

Nyut (*adj*): flash,

Nyute (*adj*): showy, proud,

Nyute (lonyo) (*adj*): luxurious,

Nyute (*n*): drive, campaign,

Nyute (*n*): show, performance,

Nyuto (*adj*): flash,

Nyuto (coco, kero) (*n*): exercise, implementation, carrying out,

Nyuto (*n*): flash,

Nyuto (*v*): imply, introduce, present, mention, notice, stage, show, signal,

Nyuto (*v*): perform, present,

Nyuto (*v*): share, communicate,

Nyuto ka maleŋ (*v*): reveal,

Nyuto lok (*v*): disclose, reveal,

Nyuto muŋ (*v*): divulge, reveal,

Nyuto nywe (*v*): flash,

Nyuto woro (*adj*): modest,

Nyuto yo (*v*): direct, show the way,

Nyuto yo laboŋ koc (*n, leg.*): procedural fairness,

Nyuto yòo (kit me poŋo gin acoya nyo nyuto gin ma kot mito) (*n, leg.*): direction,

Nywako (*adj*): cooperative,

Nywako (*n*): share,

Nywako (*v*): play, participate,

Nywako (*v*): share,

Nywal (*n*): bear, give birth, birth, delivery,

Nywal ko (*adj*): barren,

Nywalo (*v*): bore, reproduce, have a children, breed,

Nywane (*adj*): messy, stained,

Nywano cwiny dano (*adj*) agitate

Nywano lok (*v*): babble,

Nywaŋnywaŋ (*adj*): grotesque,

O

Oaa (*adj*): decided

Obab aduno (*adj*): oval,

Obale (*adj*): damaged, spoiled, deficient, faulty,

Obale woko (*adj*) damaged,

Obalo kido (*adj*): distort, disfigure,

Obaŋe oko (*adj*): vapid,

Obar (*v*): tear, crack,

Obik (*n*): monster, ogre,

Obino ki apurukudaŋ (*adj*): zealous,

Obino kwe (*adj*): belated, (*lit.*) late, delayed,

Obino maber (*adj*): positive,

Obino manyen (*adj*): fresh, original, innovative, unique,

Obiya (*n*): napier grass,

Oboke (*n*): leave,

Oburu (*adj*): warning, threatening,

Oburu (*n*): ruin,

Obwara (*n*): evening,

Obwore (*adj*): droopy, tired, worn out, fatigue, exhausted, rundown,

Obwot (*adj*): escaped,

Obwot (*n*): abandon,

Obwoto (*adj*): abandoned, deserted, forsaken, neglected, cast off, dumped,

Obwoto jwene (*adj*): disloyal,

Ocakke too (*v*): continue, resume,

Ocek (*adj*): ripe,

Ocek (*n*): ripe, cooked,

Ocek ko (*adj*): unripe,

Ocek laboŋo Acholi mede (*adj*): organic,

Ocene (*n*): grasshopper,

Ocer acera (*adv*): accidently

Ocero (*adj*): marked, striped,

Ocero ko (*adj*): unlined,

Ocero lii (*adj*): lined,

Ociko (*adj*): pointed,

Ociko rom ki wade (*adj*): harmonious,

Ocobo ko (*adj*): abortive, failed, fruitless, unproductive, futile,

Ocudi (matidi) (*adj*): knobby,

Ocune (*adj*): thick,

Ocuŋo (*adj*): calm (*lit.*) stop, (*n.*) peace,

Ocuŋo gwir (*adj*): solid,

Ocuŋo kamaleŋ (*adj*): striking,

Ocuŋo matek (*adj*): steady, firm,

Ocwee (*adj*): plump, fat, obese, fat, overweight, portly, chubby,

Ocwee ŋuru (ŋate noŋo cek) (*adj*): tubby,

Odde (*n*): jolt,

Oddo (*n*) hit,

Oddo (*v*): poke,

Oddo woko (*adj*): repulsive,

Odeŋo cwiny (*adj*): flash,

Oder (*adj*): exhausted, tired, worn,

Odero dano woko (*adj*): mundane,

Odet makwar ni nywa (*adj*): ruddy,

Odeyo makwak (*adj*): ornate,

Odii (*n*): butter (Peanut, Sesame),

Odiko (*adj*): destroyed, damaged,

Odiko (*n*): morning,

Odilo (*n*): football,

Odilo ciŋ (*n*): basketball,

Odiŋ (*adj*): defiant,

Odo (*adj*): bumpy,

Odo (*n*): smash,

Odo (*v*): smash,

Odo (wic) (*n*): bang,

Odo (wiye) (*v*): bang, hit,

Odog odog (*adj*): gummy, sticky,

Odok ma gi nyobo (calo moko magi nyobo ki pii me mwono waraga) (*n*): paste,

Odonyo i iye (*adj*) damaged, dented

Odoo (*n*): stick, whip, lash, flog,

Odoo (*n*): stroke, hit,

Odoo madit mabor (*n*): bar,

Odunyo (*adj*): polished,

Odur (*n*): rubbish,

Oduro (*n*): heap, pile,

Oduru (*n*): scream, yell,

Oduru ki dwan maliu (*n*): shriek,

Odwanye (*adj*): warped,

Odwanye malo piny (*adj*): zigzag,

Odyak (*adj*): damp, moist, humid, wet, soggy, clammy,

Odyak doki pii (*adj*): wet,

Odyak doki pii pii (*adv*): wetly,

Ogak (*v*): continue, remain,

Ogicu (*n*): spinal cord, spine,

Ogicu omako (*adj*): shocked,

Ogik (*adj*): ended, done with,

Ogik ko (*adj*): immense,

Ogiko pi tutunu (*n, leg.*): adjournment,

Ogom (*adj*): crooked, bent, curved, warp,

Ogom (*n*): bend,

Ogonyo (*n*): release, liberation,

Ogul tyelo (*n*): ankle,

Ogule (*adj*): bow, curved, curvy,

Ogulu (*v*): germinate, develop, take a root, evolve, sprout,

Oguny (*n*): monkey,

Ogure (*adj*): crowded, congested,

Ogwa (*n*): nest,

Ogwado (*adj*): damaged, scratched, scratchy,

Ogwal (*n*): frog,

Ogweto (*adj*): marked,

Ojaŋo (*adj*): neglected, abandoned, deserted, forsaken, derelict, neglected, cast off, dumped, discarded, rundown, in poor or neglected state,

Ojiŋ (*adj*): stiff, tense,

Ojiŋ (ki ŋico) *(adj)*: freezing,

Ojiŋ (ki ŋico) *(adj)*: frozen,

Ojiŋ ki koyo (*adj*): freezing, cold, sub- zero,

Ojiŋ ki ŋico (*adj*): freezing, icy, frozen,

Ojiŋ ko (*adj*): limp,

Ojony (*adj*): thin, slim,

Ojony ki ŋico (*adj*): freezing,

Ojul (*adj*): zealous, zesty,

Ojunye (*adj*): crowded, congested,

Ojunye (*adj*): thick,

Ojunye ko (*adj*): thin,

Ok (*n*): reach,

Ok (*v*): arrive, reach, arrive at,

Ok (*v*): land, settle,

Ok iwiye ko (*adj*): limited,

Okal lak (*n*): toothache,

Okane (*adj*): hidden,

Okato (*adj*): past,

Oket (*adj*): cluttered,

Oket ata (*adj*): untidy,

Oket ata (Boŋo) (*adj*): tattered,

Oket oko (*adj*): shattered,

Oketo atata (*adj*): shattered,

Oketo cwinye gobo iye (*adj*): worried, uptight, nervous

Oketo i cwiny (*adj*): marked,

Okeyo (*n*): nephew,

Oko (*adv*): away,

Oko (*prep.*): off,

Okoba akoba ko (*adj*): original,

Okono (*n*): pumpkin,

Okore (*adj*): lone, odd,

Okoro (*n*): snail,

Okube akuba (labole calo gaŋ cat madoŋo) (*adj*): complex, sets of building

Okuto (*adj*): thorny, spiky, spiny,

Okwano (*adj*): educated, well- informed, well –read, learned, scholarly, erudite, cultivated, cultured,

Okwano ko (*adj*): illiterate,

Okwe (*adj*): cool, chill,

Okweyo (*adj*): comforted, relieved, reassured, please, calmed, pleased,

Okwok (*adj*): putrid, rotten, decaying, decomposing, musty,

Okwok (kwon) (*adj*): stale,

Okwok (*n*): infection,

Okwok (*n*): rotten,

Okwor matar (*adj*): wan, pale,

Okwore matar (*adj*): pale,

Ol (*v*): tire,

Ola (*n*): pass, passage, tunnel,

Olaŋ me coyo dano (*n*): alarm,

Oliŋ (*adj*): extinct, (*lit*) calmed,

Olodo (*adj*): inferior, second –rate, second –hand, well –worn, wornout, worn, unoriginal,

Oloke (*adj*): corrupt, alter, distort,

Oloko (*adj*): distort, alter, change, misrepresent,

Olony (*adj*): rich, abounding, affluent, rich, well –off, well-to-do, flourishing, thriving, successful, booming,

Olony ko (*adj*): abortive, failed, fruitless, unproductive, futile, bungle,

Olony woko (*adj*): rich, wealthy, comfortable, well-off, well-to-do,

Oloyo (*adj*): victorious,

Oloyo (*n*): susbstitute,

Olum (*n*): rebel,

Oluma (*adj*): hero, brave

Oluŋe aduno (*adj*): spherical,

Oluŋe mapek (*adj*): massive,

Olwoke (*n*): wear,

Omaro (*n*): cousin (male),

Omedo mo iye (*adj*): embellished,

Omedo tyena ariyo (*adj*): double,

Omine (*adj*): curly, coiled, twisted, crooked,

Omine malo doki piny (*adj*): curly,

Omino (*adj*): distort, twist,

Omiyo kome iye (*adj*): volunteer, aboard, on board, committed,

Omo (*v*): tempt,

Omok (*adj*): emaciated, undernourished,

Omoko (*adj*): grounded,

Omoko diŋ (*adj*): rigid,

Omoko matek (*adj*): stable,

Omoto i kom (*n*): addiction,

Omwolo (*adj*): tame, docile, subdued,

Omwolo (yibe) (*adj*): subdued,

Onen di iye (*adj*): verifiable,

Onen koŋ (*adj*): verifiable,

Onino ko (*adj*): sleepless,

Ono (*v*): cough,

Onoŋo (*v*): deserve,

Onur ki lewic (*adv*): sheepishly,

Onweyo kome iye (*adj*): submissive, obedient,

Onwoyo anwoya (*adj*): used,

Onwoyo tyen ariyo (*n*) double,

Ony woko (*adj*): empty, clearout,

Onyo (*v*): evacuate,

Onyo (*v*): pour, spill,

Onyo (*v*): tip, tilt,

Onyo ic (*n*): abortion, miscarriage,

Onyo kom dano doki koyo (*adj*): chilly, scary,

Onyo pii (*v*): water,

Onyobe (*adj*): impure,

Onyobe ata (*adj*): rowdy, disorderly,

Onyoc (*adj*): bulge,

Onyoc madit (*adj*): bulky

Onyomo (*adj*): married,

Onyoŋo (*adj*): mushy,

Onyoŋo (*n*): squeeze, crush,

Onyuli (*adj*): bulge,

Onyuŋe (*adj*): shabby,

Onyuŋe ki doki ottii (*adj*): shabby,

Onywalo kede (*adj*): inborn,

Oŋinye (*adj*): Curly, twisted,

Oŋinye woko (*adj*): broken in pieces,

Oŋiyo iye ko (*adj*): inexperienced, inexpert,

Oŋiyo ka wot kene (*adj*): outgoing,

Oŋoko (*n*): chameleon,

Oŋolo kop ne kiloŋ (*adj*): misguided, biased,

Oŋundo macek (*adj*): rundown, brief summary,

Oŋundo wiye macek cek (*adj*): rundown, brief summary,

Oŋwek (*adj*): pattern, mixed,

Oŋwero waŋe (*adj*): glaring,

Oŋwide doki dul mapatpat (labole calo gaŋ cat madoŋo) (*adj*): complex,

Oŋwide matino tino (*n*): chip,

Oo (*n*): spill,

Ook (*n*): return,

Ool (*adj*): tired, weary, exhausted, worn out, fatigued, drained, somnolent, drowsy, disillusioned, disenchanted, fed up, jaded, worn up,

Oonyo koyo (*adj*): clumsy,

Opal (*n*): shell,

Opego (*n*): pig,

Opii (*adj*): knavish,

Opii opii (*adv*): knavishly,

Opilo ko (*adj*): uneven,

Opilo wiye (*adj*): polished,

Opito laboŋo kemikal patalaica (*adj*): organic,

Opo apoa (*adj*): puzzle, surprised,

Opoŋ (*adj*): crowded, congested, (*lit*) full,

Opoŋ (*adj*): full, occupied, jam-packed, satisfied, bursting,

Opoŋ (*adj*): thick,

Opoŋ (*adv*): fully,

Opoŋ ki gen (*adv*): upbeat, positive, optimisitic,

Opoŋ ki ur (*adj*) marvelous,

Opoŋ ki yom cwiny (*adj*): nervous, (*lit.*)full of happiness, excited, overjoy, excite, delight, stimulate, electrify, excited,

Opoŋ makwak (*adj*): jam –packed, very crowded,

Opoo (kurube) (*adj*): surprised, astonished, astounded, amazed, stunned, shocked,

Opore (*adj*): qualified, standard, normal, proper, pure, chaste, uncorrupted, impecaccble, perfect, without mistake, immaculate, perfect,

Opore (*adv*): appropriately,

Opore (*adv*): well, in a good way,

Opore (*n*): righteousness,

Opore ko (*adv*): abnormally

Opoto (*n*): fall, accident,

Opoto doki pee (*adj*): frozen, freezing,

Opoto ite cik (pi en pe oculo banya) (*adj*): default,

Opuk (*n*): tortoise,

Opwonyo (*adj*): trained,

Opye mot (*adj*): calm,

Oree (*adj*): witty,

Orego arega (*adj*): mealy,

Orem (*adj*): deficient, shortage,

Oreny (*adj*): orange,

Orii i keno (*adj*): overcooked,

Orii(*adj*): stale,

Oriyo ne too makwar (*adj*): parched,

Oroce aroca (*adv*): accidently

Oroma aroma (*adj*): innocent,

Oroma roma (*adv*): coincidentaly, accidenttaly,

Oromo (*adj*): ample, enough, plenty,

Oruco (*n, leg*): extinguish,

Orumo (*adj*): crowded, (*lit and adj*): surrounded,

Oruŋ (*n*): wrinkle,

Orwate (*adj*): proper,

Orweny (*adj*): lost,

Orweyo maleŋ (*adj*): spotless, immaculate,

Orwo (*adj*): thirsty,

Orwo (pii) (*adj*): thirsty,

Orye ki waŋ tal malii (*adj*): linear,

Oryebe piny (*adj*): flat,

Ot (*n*): shelter, housing,

Ot cat (*n*): shop,

Ot cat ma gi gwoko iye gi me cat (*n*): store

Ot koŋo (*n*): bar,

Ot matye araba (*adj*): flat,

Ot me yubo ga (*n*): factory,

Ot pa winyo (*n*): nest,

Ot tedo (*n*): kitchen,

Ot yat (*adj*): medical,

Ot yat (*n*): clinic,

Ot yat madit (*n*): hospital,

Otama atama (*adj*): imaginary,

Otaŋa (*n*): grashopper,

Otegi (*adj*): mature,

Otego marom (*n*): harmony,

Oteka (*adj*): brave, courageous, hero, legend,

Otemo ko (*adj*): untried,

Otii (*adj*): corny, (lit.) old,

Otii (*adj*): old, shabby, worn,

Otii oket taŋ taŋ (*adj*): threadbare,

Otime (*v*): happen, occur,

Otimo ki cwiny weŋ (*adj*): studious,

Otimo ki gin mo iye (gine pat apata) (*adj*): warp,

Otito ogoyo waŋ coŋe (*adj*): faint,

Otiyo kede ko (*adj*): unused,

Otono cwiny (a*dj*): monotonous,

Otono cwiny dano woko (*adj*): monotonous,

Otop (*adj*): rotten,

Otop (*n*): decay, rot,

Otore madit (*adj*): massive,

Otore mapek (*adj*): massive,

Otoro (*n*): heap, pile,

Otoro tyen ariyo (*n*): double,

Otti (*n*): wear,

Otto (*adj*): dead, deceased, departed, lifeless

Otude (*adj*): dapper, knotty,

Otum (*adj*): complete, finish, finished, over, exhausted,

Otum (*n*): end,

Otum ko (*adj*): incomplete, unfinished,

Otuŋ ki awoo (*adj*): livid,

Otur (*adj*): broken,

Otur kiji kiji (*n*): Wreck,

Otwi (*v*): germinate,

Otwi kede manyen (*adj*): novel, new,

Otwo (*adj*): dry,

Otyeno (*n*): afternoon,

Otyero (*adj*): smashed,

Oustrolia (*n*): Australia,

Owane (*adj*): damaged, injured, hurt,

Oweko (*adj*): abandoned, deserted, forsaken, derelict, neglected, cast off, dumped, discarded,

Oweko (*conj.*): so,

Oweli (*adj*): lumpy,

Owilo woko (*adj*): corrupt, bribed,

Owito (*adj*): discarded,

Oyabe (*adj*): unfolded,

Oye iye (*adj*): legitimate,

Oyec (*adj*): torn,

Oyee (*adj*): willing,

Oyenyo (*v*): deserve,

Oyeŋ (*adj*): satisfied,

Oyeŋ yeŋ (*n*): shock, tremor,

Oyero (*adj*): decided,

Oyo (v): flow, run,

Oyoge (*adj*): loose,

Oyoo (*n*): rat, mouse

Oyot (*adj*): fast, quick, prompt, rapid, speedy, urgent, swift,

Oyot oyot (*adv*): easily, quickly, urgently, rapidly, swiftly, quicker, briskly, hurriedly, fastly,

Oyotoyot (*adj*): hasty, abrupt, brisk, rapid, quick, rushed, speedily, faster, whirlwind,

Oyube maber (*adj*): efficiently, well-organized,

Oyubo ki ciŋ (*adj*): manual, handmade,

Oyubo maleŋ (*adj*): tidy,

Oywek (*adj*): Illustrious, memorable, well-known, famous, notable,

P

Pa (*prep.*): for, intended for, of,

Pa (*v*): belong,

Pa lolonyo (*adj*): lavish, luxury,

Pa lwak ko (cat, gaŋ kwan) (*adj*): private

Pa mon (*adj*): femine,

Pacoo (*adj*); masculine,

Pak (*n*): cheer,

Pako (*v*): cheer, extol,

Pala (*n*): knife,

Pam ma la tyene (*n*): skateboard,

Pam me ywire (*n*): ski,

Pamba me bur (*n*): gauze,

Panga (*n*): panga,

Pano cwiny (*n*): jolt,

Paŋe apaŋa (*adj*): corrupt, dishonest, crooked, fraudulent,

Paŋe ko (*adj*): inevitable,

Paŋo (*adj*): dodgy, dishonest, unprincipled, corrupt, crooked, immoral, deceitful, devious,

Papayi (*n*): pawpaw,

Papol (*adj*): purple,

Par (*adj*): nervous, worried, concerned, uneasy, apprehensive, restless, fretful, eager, keen, grave, concern, anxiety, worry, apprehension, fear, distress, unease, disquiet, trepidation, troubled, disturbed, bothered, anxious, afraid, alarmed, upset,

Par (*n*): worry, anxiety, care, concern, fear, trouble,

Para (*pron.*): my,

Pare (*adj*): memorable,

Paro (*v*): concern, worry, fret, trouble,

Paro (*v*): mourn,

Paro (*v*): remember,

Paro ko (*adj*): (lit.)not worry, confident, paro ko, imperturbable, sure- footed

Pat (*adj*): unique, different, distinct,

Patapata (*adj*): unique,

Patapata (ber) (*adv*): exceptionally,

Patpat (*adj*): separate, odd,

Payipayi (*n*): pawpaw,

Pe (*adj*): negative,

Pe (i yo mo keken, makwak) (*adv*): never,

Pe (kadi) (*adv*): not,

Pe ber (*adj*): unfavourable, unsuitable,

Pe calo (*prep.*): unlike,

Pe cime (*adv*): impressively,

Pe cobo (*adj*): failing,

Pe dwoŋ (*adj*): few, not many, hardly any,

Pe gi akalakala (*adj*): confident, bouncy, (lit.) no doubt,

Pe gi keto itic (*adj*): impractical,

Pe gi yubo ki ciŋ (*adj*): natural,

Pe gik (*adj*): infinite,

Pe i poro (*adj*): extraordinary,

Pe ika ciŋ (*adj*): insecure,

Pe ikit ma gi ginywalo (i) kede (*adj*): unnatural,

Pe iporo (*adv*): extraordinarily,

Pe ite cik (*adj*): unlawful, illegal, illicit, against the law, illegitimate, criminal,

Pe keto cwinye (*adj*): reluctant,

Pe ki bal (*adj*) innocent, blameless, not guilty, pure, spotless, perfect, immaculate, angelic,

Pe ki bal mo (*adv*) innocently,

Pe ki gen (*adj*): pessimistic, abject, hopeless,

Pe ki gen (*adv*): hopelessly,

Pe ki gi ciŋe (*adj*): defenseless, an armed,

Pe ki gum kom (*adj*): unfortunate,

Pe ki kala (*adj*): colourless,

Pe ki kome (*adj*): insubstantial,

Pe ki lewic (*adj*): shameless, brazen, barefce, unabashed, blatant, unashamed,

Pe ki ŋec (*adj*): unaware, ignorant, uninformed, clueless, badly informed, inexperienced, lack of experienced, skillfull, wide-eyed,

Pe ki woro (*adj*): impolite,

Pe leŋ (*adj*): impure,

Pe loke (*adj*): definite, fixed, settled, definitive, stable,

Pe mo acel (*pron.*): none,

Pe ŋol (*adj*): constant, steady, stable, even, invariable, unvarying, regular, continuous, endless,

Pe opore (*adj*): informal,

Pe pwore wa (*adv*): impressively,

Pe rac (*adj*): mild,

Pe rac (*adj*): normal,

Pe rac (labole ka ŋat ma kome lit nyo owane) (*adj*): stable,

Pe rac keket (*adj*): fair

Pe rac keket (*adv*): quite, fairly, somewhat,

Pe rwate ki lok ma gi tye kaloko ne ni (*adj*): extraneous, irrelavant, unrelated, inappropriate,

Pe tero kare (*adv*): shortly, soon,

Pe tum (*adj*): perpetual,

Pe tum (*adv*): forever,

Pe tye ada doki pe tye atir (*adj*): ethical,

Pe tye con (*adj*): unnatural,

Pe tye ikin gi (*pron.*): neither,

Pe tye kulu (*n*): fraction

Pe tye marac (*adj*): stable,

Pe yomo cwiny (*adv*): impressively,

Pe yot (*adj*): unhealthy,

Pec (*n*): drag,

Pee (*n*): hailstone, ice,

Pek (*adj*): cumbersome, heavy, bulk, weighty,

Peke (*adj*): deficient, lacking,

Peke (*adv*): away, absent, gone, missing,

Peke (*pron.*): nothing,

Peko (*adj*): poverty, poor, burden, trouble, troubled, problematic, costly, suffering,

Peko (*n*): burden, problem, matter, trouble, poverty,

Peko (*n*): question, problem,

Peko (*n*): risk,

Peko (*n*): state, condition,

Peli (*n*): pair of short (pant),

Peloke (*adj*): abiding, permanent,

Pen (*n*): umbilical cord,

Peny (*n*): challenge, question, query, examination, test,

Penye ko (*adj*): unquestionable,

Penye ko (*adv*): unquestionably,

Penyo (*v*): demand, ask, grill, question, interrogate, quiz, inquire,

Penyo koŋ (*v*): examine, test,

Penyo peny (*n*): challenge,

Penyo peny (*n, leg.*): interrogatories,

Pere (*pron.*): his, her, it,

Peri (*pron.*): yours,

Pet tye atir (*adj*): abnormal,

Pet tye atir (*adv*): abnormally,

Pet ye ŋat mo (*pron.*): nobody, no one,

Petum (*adj*): bountiful, abundant, (*lit.*) will not finish,

Peyo (*v*): tow,

Pi (*prep.*): about,

Pi (*prep.*): concerning, about, toward, for, in favour of, on behalf of, of, per, regarding,

Pi en (*conj.*): as, because, for, since,

Pi en (*prep.*) through, because of,

Pi eni (*adv*): so, consequently, as a result, thus, therefore, subsequently, hence, then, in that case, thus,

Pi eni (*conj.*): so,

Pi kare macek (*adv*): temporarily,

Pi kare malac (*adj*): long –termed,

Pi kare manok (*adv*): temporarily,

Pi pire matek (*adv*): essentially,

Pi tutunu (*adv*): temporarily,

Pi tyen lok eni (*adv*): thereby,

Pic (*n*): influence,

Pido (*n, leg.*): trail,

Pig (*adj*): fluid,

Pig dek (*n*): soup,

Pig mon (*n*): fluid from vagina,

Pig waŋ (*n*): tear,

Pii (*n*): water,

Pii ma ŋic (*n*): cold water, soft drink,

Pii ne cilo (*adj*): murky,

Pii piii (*n*): wet,

Piko (*v*): pump,

Pilm (*n*): film, movie,

Pilo (*v*): level, knock down,

Pilo wiye (*v*): gather, conclude,

Pim (*n*): test,

Pime (*adj*): measurable,

Pime ko (*adj*): immeasurable, immense,

Pime romrom (*n*): balance,

Pimo (*v*): face,

Pimo (*v*): measure, assess,

Pimo bur okoro i pyer (*n*): pap smear,

Pimo romrom (*v*): balance, calculate,

Pimo wel pa mucoro (*n, leg.*): taxation of costs,

Piny (*adj*): down, low,

Piny (*adv*): down, downward,

Piny (*prep.*): below, under, underneath,

Piny ma ŋic (*n*): freeze,

Piny oloyo (*adj*): wretched,

Pinye (*adv*): horizontally,

Piŋ (*adj*): pink,

Pire bot (*adj*): bland, insipid, tasteless, mild, featureless, dull, boring, lackluster, ordinary, unappealing, boring,

Pire ken (*adj*): sole,

Pire lit (*adj*): precious,

Pire tek (*adj*): important, principal, major, chief, prime, basic, essential, fundamental, indispensable, vital, crucial, critical, central, key, significant, vital, neccessay, noteworthy, pertinent, relavant, applicable, appropriate, required, requisite, compulsory, obligatory, mandatory, ultimate,

Pire tek (loyo weŋ) (*adv*): supreme,

Pire tek (lubo pi pwony moni) (*adj*): elementary,

Pire tek (mar, miti) (*adj*): favourite,

Pire tek (*n*): pick, choice, value,

Pire tek ko (*adj*): inconsequential, unimportant, insiginificant, trivial, petty, insignificant, negligible, minor, unnecessary, superficial,

Pire tek loyo weŋ (*adj*): primary, prime,

Pire tek makato (*adj*): valuable,

Pire tek makwak (*adj*): treasured, vital,

Piri (*n*): whistle,

Piro (*v*): grudge,

Piro waŋ (*adj*): motionless,

Piro waŋ (*n*) stare,

Piro waŋ (*v*): stare, peer,

Pito (*v*): feed, nourish, planting,

Piyo (*adj*): stimulating,

Piyo (mac) (*v*): rub,

Piyo (*v*): influence, stir, incite, screw,

Piyo bur (*v*): drill, bore,

Pluto (*n*): Pluto,

Podi (*adv*): still,

Podi obino abina (*adj*): strange,

Podi obino welo (*adj*): strange,

Poke (*adj*): scale,

Poke (*adj*): separated,

Poke (*n*): divorce, separation,

Poke (*n*): split, rip, division divide,

Poke (*v*): divorce,

Poko (*v*): divide, deal, distribute, share, split, part, separate, supply, branch,

Poko (*v*): identify, distinguish,

Poko ko (*adj*): fair,

Poko twero ikin lodoŋo me gamente (lodoŋo, loket cik ki loŋol kop) (*n, leg.*): separation of powers of doctrine,

Polo (*n*): heaven,

Poŋ (*adj*): full,

Poŋ bele bele (*n*): overflow,

Poŋ ki yom cwiny (*adj*): joyful,

Poŋ ki yom cwiny (*adv*): vivaciously,

Poŋ ki yom cwiny (*n*): thrill, kick,

Poŋ pa pii (*n*): flood,

Poŋo (*v*): fill, stuff,

Poŋo (*v*): load, overflow,

Poŋo ki alur (*v*): inflate,

Poŋo ki pii (*v*): flood,

Poo (*adj*): rash, impulse, hasty,

Poo (wic) (*adj*): shocked, surprised, stunned,

Poo apoa (ki loke, time ne) (*adj*): unruly, disruptive,

Poo iye (*v*): remember, recall,

Poo ki ajiji (*v*): shock, traumatize,

Poo wic (*n*): recall,

Pore (*adj*): perfect, righteous, classic, standard, conventional,

Pore kede (*v*): deserve,

Pore ko (*adj*): inferior, substandard, imcomparable,

Poro (*v*): compare, identify, associate,

Poro (*v*): copy,

Poro dog (*v*): quote, cite,

Poru (*adj*): arid,

Poru (*adj*): bare, desert, barren,

Poru (*n*): desert,

Pot (*adj*): page, leaf,

Pot (*n*): page,

Potapota (*adj*): flaky, coming off,

Pote (yat) (*adj*): leafy,

Poto (*n*): drop, descent, fall, reduction,

Poto (*n*): farm, garden,

Poto (*v*): drop, fall,

Poto (*v*): fail, unsuccessful,

Poto (*v*): fall, tumble,

Poto (*v*): freeze,

Poto doki pee (*v*): snow,

Poyo (*v*): remember, recall,

Poyo pire (*v*): notice,

Poyo wic (*adj*): evocative,

Poyo wic (*v*): grip, affect somebody or something greatly,

Poyo wic (*v*): remember, remind, tell again, recall,

Prenc (*adj*): French,

Pudi (*adj*): just, only, still,

Pudi (*adv*): yet,

Pukko cwiny (*v*): envy,

Pul (*n*): peanut,

Pund punda (col piny) (*adj*): dim,

Pundi (*n*): mechanic, technician,

Pundi madit (*n*): engineer,

Puŋ (*adj*): close, block, closed

Puŋo (*v*): close, seal, zip, lock,

Pur (*n*): dig,

Pur (*v*): farm, cultivate,

Pure doki cilo (*adj*): grimy,

Puro (*v*): dig, break up earth, garden, plow,

Puyo ki daab (*v*): gild,

Pware (*adj*): gleeful, merry,

Pware (*n*): dare, challenge,

Pwoc (*adj*): thanks, grateful, thankful,

Pwod (*n*): discipline, punishment,

Pwodo (*v*): punish, chastise, discipline,

Pwol (*n*): buttock,

Pwol (*n*): cloud,

Pwol pwol (*adj*): cloudy,

Pwony (*adj*): uplifiting,

Pwony (*n*): lecture,

Pwonye (*n*): practice, rehearsal, exercise,

Pwonye ko (*adj*): wild, undisplined,

Pwonye magi nwoya anwoya (calo pwonyo lomwony) (*n*): drill, practice, train,

Pwonyo (*adj*): instructive, educational, informative,

Pwonyo (juko) (*v*): reprimand, chastise,

Pwonyo (*v*): coach, train, teach, instruct, learn, educate, lecture, prepare,

Pwonyo dore (*v*): drill,

Pwore wa (*adj*): impressive,

Pwot (*adj*): greasy, slippery, slimy, smooth,

Pwot menyo amenya calo tol obuceŋ (*adj*): silky,

Pwot nionio (ikala, dwan, i bilo ga) (*adj*): mellow,

Pwot pa dwan (*adj*): silky,

Pwot runyu runyu (*adj*): mellow,

Pwoyo (*adj*): thankful,

Pwoyo (*n*): scar,

Pwoyo (*v*): appreciate,

Pwoyo (*v*): hail, acclaim,

Pwoyo (*v*): thank,

Pwoyo adada (*v*): rave,

Pwoyo bero (*n*): mention,

Pwoyo ko (*adj*): disapproving, damaging, negative (lit). not thanking,

Pye (*adj*): bouncy,

Pye (mot) (*v*): settle, become peaceful,

Pye (*n*): jump, bounce, hop, leap,

Pye (*v*): hop, jump, skip,

Pye doki dal (*v*): bounce,

Pye doki del del (*adj*): bumpy,

Pye doki del del (*v*): bob,

Pye mot (*adj*): calm,

Pye mot (*v*): relax,

Pye piny (*v*): settle, sink,

Pyelo (*v*): lay,

Pyem (*n*): challenge, dispute, argument, battle, debate, fray,

Pyeme ko (*adj*): genuine, real, authentic, indisputable, true, unadulterated, legitimate, valid, actual,

Pyemo (*adj*): opposite,

Pyemo (ituko) (*v*): race,

Pyemo (*v*) challenge, dispute, compete, counter, oppose, fight,

Pyemo ki (*adj*): opposite,

Pyemo ŋoc (pa ŋat mu doto ki ŋat ma bolo doge) (*n, leg.*): counter claim,

Pyera abic (*n*): fifty,

Pyera abic wiye acel (*n*): fifty one,

Pyera abiro (*n*): seventy,

Pyera abiro wiye acel (*n*): seventy one,

Pyera aboŋwen (*n*): ninety,

Pyera aboŋwen wiye acel (*n*): ninety one,

Pyera aboro (*n*): eighty,

Pyera aboro wiye acel (*n*): eighty one,

Pyera adek (*n*): thirty,

Pyera adek wiye acel (*n*): thirty one,

Pyera aŋwen (*n*): fourty,

Pyera aŋwen wiye acel (*n*): fourty one,

Pyera ariyo (*n*): twenty,

Pyera ariyo wiye acel (*n*): twenty one,

R

Raa (*n*): hippopotamus,

Raba ka (*adj*): flat,

Rac (*adj*): bad, awful, terrible, dreadful, appalling, shocking, ghastly, horrific, dire, unpleasant, evil, dangerous, unsafe, hazardous, risky, perilous, dodgy, treacherous, ugly, nasty, wicked, immoral,

Rac (*n*): risk,

Rac cwiny (*adj*) ruthless,

Rac kit (*adj*): wicked, corrupt, immoral, depraved, debauched, unscrupulous, ruthless, merciless, cruel, rude,

Rac makwak (*adj*): awful, worst, terrible,

Rac makwak (*adj*): worse,

Rac makwak (*adv*): awfully,

Radiyo (*n*): radio,

Rat rat (*adj*): flat

Rec (*n*): fish,

Rek (*n*): line, order,

Rek ma riŋo lii kacel ento kin gi opoke woko maromrom (*adj*): parallel,

Rek ma tye arii (*n*): row,

Rek ma yute piny doki dok malo (*adj*): squiggly,

Remo (*adj*): painful,

Remo (*n*): blood,

Remo ko (*adj*): painless,

Remo makwak (*adj*): painful,

Rep (*adj*): breakable, fragile, delicate, brittle, frail, (*lit.*) weak, flaw, weakness, flimsy, frail, puny, thin,

Rep pel pel (*adv*): dainty,

Ret (*n*): bur, fresh wound, injury,

Ribbi (*n*): join,

Ribe (*adj*): united,

Ribe (*v*): unite,

Ribo (*adj*): calculating, coordinate,

Ribo (*v*): add, combine, include, incorporate,

Ribo (*v*): attach, connect,

Ribo (*v*): juggle,

Ribo (*v*): merge,

Rido (*adj*): tight,

Rido (*n*): chip,

Rido dwan (*n*): screech,

Rii (*adj*): last, delayed, late, abiding, long lasting, remaining, lasting,

Rii (*n*): pole,

Rii (*v*): impress, emphasize,

Rii (*v*): last, span,

Rii kec (*n*): fast,

Rii ki kec *(v)*: fast,

Rii ko (*adv*): shortly, soon,

Rii makwak (*adj*): long lasting,

Riŋo (ki i wi yamo) (*v*): fly,

Riŋo (*n*): run, trot,

Riŋo (*n*): meat,

Riŋo (*v*): run, flee

Riŋo ariŋa ki wot (*v*): trot,

Riŋo ma moo pe iye (*adj*): lean,

Riŋo riŋo (*adj*): meaty,

Riyo (*adj*): demanding, insistent,

Riyo (lok) (*adj*): persistent, insistent, adamant,

Riyo (lok) (*n*): insisit,

Riyo (*v*): assert, maintain, demand, insist, be adamant,

Riyo (*v*): bandage, dress, bind up,

Riyo (*v*): curl,

Riyo (*v*): press, pursue, insist on, swear,

Riyo (*v*): winding,

Riyo lok (*n*): barrage,

Riyo lok (*v*): barrage,

Riyo moro koko pa muduku (*n*): barrage,

Roc (*n*): molt,

Roco (*v*): molt,

Rok (*adj*): exotic,

Rok wade (*n*): peer,

Rok wiye (*n*): adult hood, child hood,

Rom (*adj*): common,

Rom (*adj*): common, equal, identical, same, similar, uniform,

Rom (kede, ki en) (*adj*): worthy,

Rom (*prep.*) near, like,

Rom ki (*adv*): equally,

Rom ki (*prep.*): like,

Rom ki ŋit (*n*): computer,

Rom ki wel nyo ca ma otiyo kede (*adj*): worthwile,

Rom ko (*adj*): uncommon, unequaled, incomparable, unique, unrivaled, unsurpassed, beyond compare, unmatched, abnormal, irregular, anomalous, odd, peculiar, uneven, (*lit*) not the same, bumpy,

Roma aroma (*adv*): uniformally,

Roma roma (*adj*): uniform, common, normal, ordinary consistent, standardized, homogeneous, identical, unvarying, even, regular, the same, equal, harmonized, even,

Romo (*adj*): qualified,

Romo (*adv*): sufficient,

Romo (*v*): meet,

Romo wano (*adj*): harmful,

Romrom (*n*): balance,

Rore (*n*): inflammation, inflammatory,

Rore pa abor (*n*): bronchitis,

Rore pa abyero (*n*): cystitis,

Roto (*v*): snoop, spy,

Roto waŋ (*v*): Peer,

Royo (*n*): insert,

Royo (*v*): add, insert, fit, fix, install, inject,

Royo (*v*): plug,

Royo dog (*n*): heat, spicy hotness,

Royo i buc (*v*): Jail,

Royo ŋec (calo i waraga me lok angeya) (*n*): insert,

Rubat (*n*): bandage, dressing,

Rube (*n*): prick,

Rube (wic) (*adj*): confused, (*lit*) mixing,

Rube pa wic (*adj*): stress,

Rubiya (*n*): money,

Rubo (*adj*): mixed,

Rubo (*n*): stir, mix,

Rubo (*v*): mix,

Rubo (*v*): stir,

Rubo wic (*adj*): puzzle, confuse, bewilder, perplex, baffle, mystify,

Rubo wic (*v*): confused,

Rubu wi dano (*adj*): complicated, confusing,

Ruc (*n*): rice,

Ruce ko (*adj*): indelible, impossible to remove,

Ruco (*v*): spray,

Ruda (*n*): gazelle,

Rude (*n*): friction,

Rudi (*adj*): twin,

Rudi (*n*): twin,

Rudo (*n*): scrape,

Rudu (*adj*): gripping,

Ruk (*n*): wear, attire,

Ruko (*v*): wear, dress, get dressed,

Rumo (lomwony) (*v*): besiege,

Rumo (*v*): surround,

Rumo kom (*v*): fence,

Ruyo (*adj*): snappy, hasty,

Ruyo lok (*v*): jabber,

Rwate (dako ki laco,) (*v*): mate,

Rwate (*n*): fit, match,

Rwate (*v*): concur, fit, match, suit,

Rwate ki lok moni (*v*): rhyme,

Rwate ko (*adj*): incompatible, extraneous, irrelevant, unrelated, chilly, (*lit*) not compatible,

Rwatte (*n*): contact,

Rweny (*v*) lose, fade, lose, misplace, stray,

Rweny ko (*adj*): indelible, unforgettable,

Rwenyo (kwo,) (*n*): cost,

Rwenyo (kwo,) (*v*): cost,

Rwere (boŋo murweyo) (*n*): fold,

Rweyo kom (*n*): massage,

Rwo (*adj*): regret,

Rwom (*adj*): level, grand, distinguished,

Rwom (*n*): postion, rank, place, self- esteem,

Rwom ma malo (*adj*): lofty,

Rwom ma malo (*adj*): superior, high –level,

Rwom ma orwate ki rwodi (*adj*): royal,

Rwom pere piny (*adj*): inferior, lower, junior, poor,

Rwot (*n*): chief,

Rye rye (*adv*): suddenly,

Ryebe (*adj*): lying flat,

Ryee (*adv*): specially, specifically,

Ryee ne (*adv*); particular,

Ryek (*adj*): bright, intelligent, clever, smart, brainy, sharp, shrewd, cute, prudent, sensible, careful, cautious, discreet, wise, quaint, crafty and plotting, witty,

Ryek (*adv*): cutely,

Ryek (*n*): sense, intelligence,

Ryeko –bwola (*adj*): crafty, cunning,

Ryem (*n*): chase,

Ryemo (*v*): fire, dismiss, chase, expel, sack, dismiss,

Ryeny (*adj*): dazzling, glaring, radiant,

Ryeny (*adj*): sunny, clear,

Ryeny (*n*): shining,

Ryeny pa la kalatwe (*adj*): starry,

Ryereye (*adv*): immediately

Ryerye (*adj*): immediate, automatic, rapid, hasty, quick, rushed, sudden, unexpected, abrupt, swift, hast, impulsive,

Ryerye (*adv*): immeadiately,

Ryeyo (*v*): arrange, organize, list,

T

Taa (*n*): tobacco, cigarette,

Taa maraco (*n*): drug,

Taco lok (*adj*): candid, frank, open, honest, truthful, sincere, blunt, straight, outspoken, straightforward,

Taco lok atir iwi dano (*adj*): forthright, upfront, straightforward, direct, frank, outspoken, plainspoken,

Tai (*n*): tie,

Tam (*adj*): intent, intention, aim, goal, target, objective, plan,

Tam (*adj*): thought, concerned, decision,

Tam (*n*): comment, criticism, remark,

Tam (*n*): hint, tip,

Tam (*n*): position, opinion, stand, attitude,

Tam (*n*): program, plan,

Tam (*n*): sneeze,

Tam dano (*adj*): considerate,

Tam iye matut (*adj*): realistic, sensible, pragmatic, practical, down-to-earth, levelhead, reasonable, rational,

Tam me wic (*adj*): fancy, (*lit.*), thought ,

Tam oyot (*adj*): imaginative,

Tam pa laŋol kop (*n, leg.*): judicial discretion,

Tamo (*adj*): decided,

Tamo (*v*): comment, remark, consider, imagine, expect, label, notice, perceive, plan, suppose,

Tamo (*v*): think,

Tamo i lok (*v*): frame,

Tamo iye (*n, leg.*): discretion,

Tamo iye (*prep.*): considering, consider, examine, form, conceive of something,

Tamo iye (*v*): invent,

Tamo iye (*v*): reflect, theorize, weigh,

Tamo iye matut (*adj*): thoughtful,

Tamo ko (*adj*): carefree, easy-going, mindless, thoughtless,

Tamo lok (*v*): postulate, assume,

Tamo lok ikom (*adj*): suspicious, suspect, wary, distrustful, circumspect, mistrustful, guarded,

Tamo lok ikom (ngat mo) (*v*): suspect,

Tamo matidi (*adj*): petty, small-minded,

Tamo matut (*v*): ponder,

Tamo ni gimo maber time manoŋo pe timo (*adj*): idealistic, unrealistic,

Tane (*adj*): poised, wiggle,

Tane (Goyo gog) (*v*): shrug,

Tane (*n*): pride

Tanne (*adv*): wiggly,

Taŋu (*n*) miracle, wonder, magic,

Tar (*adj*): white,

Tar rippi rippi (*adj*): gray,

Tara (*n*): light,

Taritari (*adj*): abnormal, unusual, deviant, anomalous, peculiar, irregular, atypical, aberrant,

Taritari (*adv*): abnormally,

Taro (*adj*): gleaming, luminous,

Taro (*v*): sparkle,

Taro waŋ (*v*): ogle,

Tat tat (kec, wac) (*adj*): tart

Tawa (*n*): pan,

Tayi (*cuŋo*): pokerfaced, straight –faced,

Te (*n*): supply, source,

Te cik (*n, leg.*): custom,

Te lak (*n*): gums

Te layot (*n*): armpit,

Te nino ni (*adj*): current, present,

Te twero (*n*): rule,

Tedo (*n*): cooking, cookery,

Tedo (*v*): cook, make,

Tedo wic (*adj*): creative, inventive, imaginative, innovative,

Tege (*v*): balance, maintain equilibrium,

Tego (*v*): set, adjust,

Tek - yelo wi dano (*adj*): cumbersome, complicated, problematic,

Tek (*adj*): energetic, strong, powerful, difficult, firm, solid, hard, rigid, dense, compact, stiff, hard, mighty, stern, strong, tough, tricky, strong,

Tek (*adj*): expensive

Tek (*adv*): mighty,

Tek (icoc ki Kwan) (*adj*): flowery, elaborate,

Tek ciŋ (*adj*): austere, austerity, thrifty, frugal, economical,

Tek cwiny (*adj*): brave, courage, courageous, intrepid, fearless, valiant,

Tek cwiny (*n*): balance,

Tek cwiny me miŋo (*adj*): foolhardy,

Tek ko (*adj*): elementary,

Tek me niaŋo ne (*adj*): murky, obscure,

Tek me noŋo ne (*adj*): hard –to –find,

Tek me yene (*adj*): incredible, hard to believe, unbelievable, implausible,

Tek wic (*adj*): intrepid, adventurous, bold,

Tekwaro (*adj*): traditional,

Tekwaro (*n*): practice, custom,

Tekwaro pa logrik (*adj*): classical,

Tele (*n*): tug, pull,

Telo (*adj*): elated, erected

Telo (*adj*): leading,

Telo (tol) (*v*): tug,

Telo (*v*): guide, direct,

Telo (*v*): lead,

Telo (*v*): pull, stretch,

Telo ko (dako keken) (*adj*): frigid,

Telo lok (*n*): discourse,

Telo peke (kilo) (*v*): weigh,

Telo yoo (*v*): head, come first,

Teme (*adj*): trying,

Teme (*n*): move, attempt,

Teme (*n*): challenge, test, try,

Temo (*v*): attempt,

Temo (*v*): challenge, test, try, check,

Temo i (*adj*): tempting,

Tene (*adj*): lean, rest, prop, supported, bend over,

Tene (*v*): depend, lean, rely,

Teŋe (*n*): frame, border,

Teŋe (*n*): surround,

Ter (*adj*): burden, lumber,

Ter (*n*): anus,

Ter (*n*): burden, load,

Tere (*adj*): ready,

Tere tere (*adv*): habitually, frequently,

Teretere (*adj*): frequently, often, regularly, normally, commonly, recurrently, habitually, repeatedly,

Teretere (*adv*): often,

Teretere (*n*): tractor,

Teretere ko (*adj*): intermittent,

Tero (*v*): deliver,

Tero (*v*): drive, take,

Tero (*v*): transport,

Tibo (*n*): shade,

Tic (*n*): act, action, work, labour, job,

Tic ce pe (*adj*): trivial,

Tic ki lok *(n)*: verb,

Tic laboŋo cik (*n, leg.*): ultra vires,

Tic ma gi tiyo (*n*): record, past performance,

Tic magi miyo (*n*): exercise, assignment,

Tic pere pe (*adj*): immaterial,

Ticat (*n*): T-shirt,

Tice pe (*adj*): inferior, substandard, negligible, inisignificant, worthless,

Tice pe (ŋec nyo kwan ma lotiyo kede ko) (*adj*): rusty, out of practice,

Tice tye (*adj*): nifty,

Tidi (*adj*): little, paltry, petite, small,

Tidi (ŋit wiye) (*adj*): shallow,

Tidi (tino) (*adj*): young,

Tidi keket (*adj*): slight,

Tidi ki (*prep.*): below, less than, beneath,

Tidi ki ire (*adj*): junior,

Tidi ki liŋ diut (*adj*): miniature, tiny, wee,

Tidi rye (*adj*): negligible, tiny, small,

Tik (*n*): cheek,

Tik bunyo (ocwere matar) (*adj*): wan,

Tim (*n*): desert,

Time cok cok (*adj*): periodic,

Time doki kalukalu (kom) (*adj*): hysterical,

Time me kom marac ma bino pi cwiny ature (*n*): hayfever,

Time ni gur (*v*): gurgle,

Time pere marac (*adj*): ignorant, rude, bad-mannered, ill-mannered, impolite, ill-bred, inconsiderate, boorish,

Timo (ga, cam pere) ki di woo (*adj*): nocturnal,

Timo (*v*): practice, do,

Timo (*v*): treat, behave toward,

Timo aber (*n*): taunt,

Timo aber (*v*): taunt,

Timo aloka aloka (*v*): change, alter, develop, improve, polish,

Timo apopora (*v*): act, pretend,

Timo kica (*v*): excuse, forgive, spare, show mercy, sympathize,

Timo kom marac (*n*): allergy,

Timo oyoto (*v*): hurry,

Timo ryeko (i ayub mo keken) (*adj*): politics,

Timo tuko tuko *(adj)* flippant, jokey,

Tin (*adv*): today,

Tino (*adj*): frugal, thrifty, economical, penny-wise, tight, stingy, meager, parsimonious, sparing, careful, austerity,

Tiŋ (dano, mutukaria) (*n*): lift,

Tiŋ (*n*): carry,

Tiŋ malo (rwom) (*adj*): exalted,

Tiŋe wa (*adj*): portable,

Tiŋo (*v*): carry, lift, raise,

Tiŋo (*v*): snatch,

Tiŋo ciŋ (*v*): wave,

Tiŋo ne mit (*adj*): cuddly

Tiŋo nyiŋ (*adj*): magnificent, zealous,

Tipo (*n*): shade, shadows,

Tipo oumo woko doki tit (*adj*): shadowy,

Tipo pa dano madwogo (*adj*): haunted,

Tipo tipo (*adj*): shadowy,

Tipo wiye pe (*adj*): clumsy,

Tire kede too (*adj*): usable,

Tiro (*v*): correct, edit,

Tiro ka bal (*n, leg.*): remedy redress,

Tiro ne lii (*v*): align,

Tito (*v*): describe, explain, inform,

Tito lok (*v*): preach, lecture, sermonize, speak, discourse, deliver an address, address, give sermon,

Tito nyiŋ gi mo keken (*n*): adjective,

Tiyo (*adj*): active, aged, functional, valid,

Tiyo (*v*): act, work,

Tiyo (*v*): fray, wear out,

Tiyo (*v*): run, serve, work,

Tiŋo kede (*adj*): utilized,

Tiŋo kede (*v*): handle, control,

Tiŋo kede (wil): spend,

Tiŋo kene (*adj*): automatic

Tiyo ki lanen me lakwany (-) (*adj*): negative,

Tiyo ki ŋit pere ko (*adj*): obedient, loyal, (*lit.*) not using his mind,

Tiyo ki wiye ko (*adj)*: obedient,

Tiyo ko (*adj*): broken, dead, inactive, down, out of action, idle,

Tiyo ko (*v*): fail, stop working,

Tiyo maber (*adj*): efficiently,

Tiyo tic madwoŋ (*adj*): busy,

Tok (*n*): back of the head, back,

Tol aduno ma tiŋo remo (*n*): vein,

Tol ma dwele dwele (*n*): strap,

Tol me jwayo kin lak (*n*): floss,

Ton (*n*): drip, drop, droplet,

Ton (*n*): spot, mark,

Ton cwiny (*adj*): depressed, heartfelt, hearty, agonize,

Ton pa cilo (*n*): blot,

Tongweno (*n*): cock,

Tono (koŋo) (*n*): concentrate,

Tono (*v*): blot,

Tono (*v*): brew,

Tono (*v*): drip, drop,

Toŋ (winyo) (*n*): peck,

Toŋo (*adj*): cutting,

Toŋo (*v*) bite,

Toŋo (winyo) (*v*): peck,

Too (*adj*): dead,

Too (*adv*): again

Too (*n*): death,

Too (*n*): fox,

Too (*v*): die,

Too (*v*): puncture, deflate,

Too ijwene (*adj*): obedient,

Too waŋ (*adj*): blind,

Too waŋ (*n*): blind,

Top (*adj*): rotten, biodegradable, decay, rot, decompose,

Tor (*n*): rise, hill,

Toro (*adj*): negligence, careless,

Toro (*v*): accumulated, (*adj*), great

Toro (*v*): heap, pile,

Toro tok (*v*): expel,

Toro tyen ariyo (*v*): double,

Toyo (*n*): humid,

Trwero (*n*): dictate, command,

Tuc (*n*): injection,

Tuc (*v*): appear, rise, (sun),

Tuco (lok) (*v*): assert,

Tuco (lok) (*v*): proclaim, state publicly,

Tuco (*n*): poke,

Tuco (*n*): dig, poke, excavation,

Tuco (pii, ngom) (*v*): bore,

Tuco (*v*): admit,

Tuco (*v*): announce, post,

Tuco (*v*): inject, jab, poke, make a hole, prick, pierce, hole on a cloth, puncture,

Tuco bur (*v*): drill, bore,

Tuco ka maleŋ (*v*): declare, plead, avow, affirm,

Tucu (*adj*): piercing,

Tude ka kwoto pe (*adj*): dapper, neat

Tudo (*n*): knot,

Tudo (*v*): Knot,

Tugi (*pron.*): their,

Tugo (mac) (*n*): control, start,

Tuka atuka (*adj*): frivolous, playful, thoughtless,

Tukeno (*n*): local stove, stove

Tuko (*n*): exercise, play, match, race, contest, recreation,

Tuko (*v*): exercise, play,

Tuko (*v*): play, have fun, fool around,

Tuko a tuka (*v*): jest, joke,

Tuko ki wi dano (*adj*): politics,

Tuko ko (*adj*): serious, somber,

Tuko tuko (*n*): jest, joke,

Tuko tuko (timo ga) (*adj*): trifling,

Tula (*n*): owl,

Tulo (*v*): tip, tilt,

Tum ko (*adv*): endlessly,

Tum pa cabit (*n*): weekend,

Tun (yet) (*n*): vagina,

Tuŋ (*adj*): specific,

Tuŋ (pi ŋat mo nyo dul pa dano, ka mi dwar) (*n*): preserve,

Tuŋ (pire, pigi) (*adj*): private,

Tuŋ ki nyero (ŋala) hoot,

Tuŋ pi (*adj*): exclusive, private,

Tuŋe aŋwen pime weŋ maromrom (*adj*): Square,

Tur (*adj*): steep, dune,

Tur (*adj*): broken,

Tur (*n*): break, fracture, broken,

Tur (*n*): dune, hill, ridge, mound,

Tur (*n*): ruin,

Tur (*v*): fail, go out of the business,

Tur oyoto (*adj*): breakable, fragile, delicate, brittle, frail, precious

Tur pa cwiny (*n*): jolt,

Tur wic (*n*): face,

Ture (*adj*): elegant,

Ture (*n*): pride,

Turmuc (*n*): thermos,

Turo (*adj*): abrupt, sudden, sharp,

Turo (*adv*): puzzle,

Turo (*v*): break,

Turo (*v*): flower, bloom, flourish,

Turo cik (*adj*): illegal,

Turo cwiny (*adj*): poignant,

Turo dano (*v*): jolt,

Turo dano atura (*adj*): untimely, brusque, abrupt,

Turo doki bwa (*v*): snap,

Tut (*adj*): deep,

Tut (*n*): pus, thrush,

Tut ko (*adj*): shallow,

Tuti (*adj*): effort,

Tuti (*n*): bid, attempt,

Tuti (*v*): control, manage, wrestle,

Tutunu (*adj*): temporary,

Tutunu (*adv*): meantime,

Tutwal ne (*adv*): especially, particular,

Tuwa (*pron.*): our,

Tuwu (*pron.*): yours,

Twako (mac, dwan) (*v*): radiate,

Twenye (*n*): stretch,

Twere (*adj*): possible,

Twere (*n*): tie,

Twere ko (*adj*): cumbersome, impossible, indubitable, tricky,

Twero (*adj*): able, competent, capable,

Twero (*adj*): pontential, responsible,

Twero (*adj*): qualified,

Twero (*n*): leave, permission,

Twero (*n*): command, authority, control, rule, power, dictate, grasp, order,

Twero (*n*): handle,

Twero (*v*): afford,

Twero ko (*adj*): unfit, incompetent, incapable,

Twero ma omiyo bot kot me winyo bako dog pi lok moni (*n, leg.*): appelate jurisdiction,

Twero ma petum (*adj*) absolute, unlimited power,

Twero magi coyo me kwayo bank me culo kit wel moni (*n*): draft,

Twero me ŋolo lok ma rom ki dul me lok ma yaŋ con tye kakare (twero en myero obin ki bot laŋol kop) (*n, leg.*): precedents judgment, precedents,

Twero me poro ga (*n, leg.*): copy right,

Twero me waco lok (*n*): say, right to be heard,

Twero me winyo lok mukwoŋo (*n, leg.*): original jurisdicition,

Twero pa dano (*n, leg.*): human rights,

Twero pa kot me keto cik (*n, leg.*): jurisdicition,

Twero weŋ (*adj*): powerful,

Tweyo (cik) (*n*): ban, prohibit,

Tweyo (cik) (*v*): ban, prohibit,

Tweyo (meli, dege,) (*v*): moor,

Tweyo (tol) (*v*): fasten,

Tweyo (*v*): bolt, fasten,

Tweyo (*v*): tie, bolt,

Tweyo kacel (calo dyaŋ me pur) (*v*): harness,

Tweyo rubat (*n*): dressing,

Twi (*v*) decide,

Twi (*v*): rise, originate,

Twi (*v*): shoot, start to grow, sprout

Twi ki lok oyoto (*adj*): decisive,

Twi ki lok wiye wiye (*adj*): quixotic,

Two (*adj*): sick, ill, unwell, unhealthy,

Two (*n*): sickness,

Two acaŋa (*adj*): medical,

Two aduno (*n*): heart condition,

Two cukari (*n*): diabetes,

Two jonyo (*n*): AIDS/HIV,

Two ki lyeto (*adj*): parch,

Two ma donyo i del magwoko ŋit ki ki ogicu (*n*): mengisitis,

Two ma kobe akoba ki idi yamo ma royo um, dwan ki lokoro (*n*): diphtheria,

Two ma kobe akoba ma coyo kom dano ki lyeto marac (*n*): measles,

Two ma kobe ki nino (*n*): shiphilis,

Two ma kweyo dano akweya (*n*): polio,

Two ma mako lac (*n*): urinary tract infection

Two ma nya ki nino (*n*): venereal disease, sexual transmitted disease,

Two ma royo cwiny aroya (*n*): hepatitis,

Two ma rweyo dano arweya doki tuŋo yweyo atuŋa (*n*): tetanus,

Two nino (*n*): sleeping sickness,

Two nino ma ŋulo tut ma royo nyim mon ki coo aroya (*n*): ghonorhea,

Two tako (*n*): appendix,

Two yweyo (*n*): asthmatic,

Twodo (*adj*): bogus, false, fake, counterfeit, phony, trick, sham, spurious, mock,

Twodo (*adj*): false, lie, untrue, lying, dishonesty,

Twodo (*n*): lie, lying, deceitful,

Twodo (*v*): lie,

Twol (*n*): snake,

Twolo (*adj*): open, vacant, empty, available, unoccupied, not in use, unfilled, not taken, free, blank, bare,

Twolo (bur) (*adj*): hollow,

Twolo waŋ (*adj*): vigilant, watchful, wide-eyed,

Twome (pii, yamo) (*adj*): turbulent,

Twomo (*v*): fetch,

Twon (coc) (*adj*): voluminous,

Twon abura (*adj*): stormy,

Twon bunyo (*n*): beam,

Twon dyaŋ (*n*): bull,

Twon kuc (*adj*): luxurious,

Twon oita lweny (*adj*): giant,

Twon yamo (*adj*): stormy,

Tworo (*n*): snore,

Tworo (*v*): snore,

Twoyo (*v*): dry,

Tye (*adj*): positive,

Tye (*adj*): present,

Tye (*adv*): there,

Tye (*v*): exist,

Tye (*v*): possess, have, own,

Tye ata ata (*adv*): hapazhardly, randomly,

Tye atir (*adj*) prim, respectable,

Tye atir ko (*adv*): wrongly,

Tye ber (*adj*): respectable,

Tye bidabid (*adj*): sticky,

Tye calo (*v*): like,

Tye cukar cukar, (*adj*): sugary,

Tye doki bur (*adj*): bumpy,

Tye doki cak cak (*adj*): milky,

Tye doki coc magi tamo iye doki tyeŋ (*adv*): poetically,

Tye doki coto (*adj*): muddy,

Tye doki dabu (*adj*): golden,

Tye doki gi makwo (*adj*): organic,

Tye doki got got (*adj*): mountainous,

Tye doki ka me poyo wic (*adj*): monumental,

Tye doki kite (*adv*): habitually,

Tye doki kwano tyeŋ nyo buk matito pilok mo (*adv*): poetically,

Tye doki kwok pere (*v*): earn, deserve,

Tye doki laber (*adv*): graciously,

Tye doki laruc (*adj*): rubbery,

Tye doki latin (*adj*): juvenile,

Tye doki latyer (*v*): star,

Tye doki lwoc (*adj*): misty,

Tye doki nyonyo (*adj*): metallic,

Tye doki obibi (*adj*): monstrous,

Tye doki pee (*adj*): icy,

Tye doki pige (*adj*): juicy, soupy,

Tye doki pii (*adj*): liquid, watery, moist,

Tye doki tipo (*adj*): shady,

Tye doki welo (*adj*): quaint, strange, peculiar, odd, bizarre, weird, extraordinary, unusual,

Tye doki yamo (*adj*): windy, blustery, breezy, story,

Tye doki yat (*adj*): wooden,

Tye dul pa dano magi timo ga tugi i muŋ (calo lokwo) (*v*): riged,

Tye dwele dwele (tol) (*v*): strap,

Tye i rom rome (*v*): level,

Tye i te cik, ikit ma pe rac nyo ber (*adj*): moral,

Tye i twon kuc (*adj*): plush,

Tye ika ciŋ (*adj*): secure,

Tye ikin wade (*adj*): aboard, on board, on the team

Tye ikit ma (*v*): depend,

Tye itam (*adj*): imaginary,

Tye ite cik (*adj*): legal, lawful, officially, permitted, authorized,

Tye ite twero (*adj*): dependent,

Tye ite twero (*adj*): inferior, lesser,

Tye iye (*v*): consist, include,

Tye ka ciŋe (*adv*): handily,

Tye ka waco (*v*): mean,

Tye ka waŋ (*adj*): ablaze, on fire, burning,

Tye kakare (*adj*): kosher, right,

Tye kakare (*adv*): exactly, genuinely,

Tye kakare ko (*adv*): wrongly,

Tye kamaleŋ (*adj*): definite, clearly stated,

Tye kede (*v*): have, possess,

Tye ki (*v*): contain, hold,

Tye ki cene ma oliŋ ki itac (*v*): fold, go bankrupt,

Tye ki cwiny (*adj*): hearty, enthuasiastic and friendly,

Tye ki cwiny (*v*): propose, intend, mean,

Tye ki gen (*adj*): upbeat, optimistic,

Tye ki gi me kwanyo kala (*v*): bleach,

Tye ki gimo ikome (*adj*): aberrant, abnormal,

Tye ki kero (*adj*): pontential,

Tye ki lok (*prep.*): against, in opposition to,

Tye ki miti (*adj*): eager, keen, zealous,

Tye ki miti (*adv*): fervently, passionately,

Tye ki miti (*v*): admire,

Tye ki miti (*v*): interest,

Tye ki miti me (*adj*): intent, concentrating, absorbed, focused, keen,

Tye ki miti me kom (*v*): desire,

Tye ki ŋec (*adj*): educated, cultured, sophisticated, urbane, knowledgeable, well –informed, skilled, expert,

Tye ki peko (*v*): risk,

Tye ki riŋo ma orude (*v*): broil,

Tye ki rwom pa rwodi (*adj*): royal,

Tye ki tam (*v*): propose, suggest,

Tye ki waŋ ma odet makwar (ki lewic, yom cwiny) (*v*): blush,

Tye ki yom cwiny mamito neko nek (*v*) excite,

Tye ladyere (*adj*): mediocre,

Tye ladyere dyere (*adj*): mild,

Tye maber (*adj*): abounding, affluent, rich, well –off, well-to-do, flourishing, thriving, successful, booming,

Tye maber (*adv*): well, favourably,

Tye macan (*adv*): woefully,

Tye manok (*adv*): finitely, limited,

Tye marac (*adj*): critical, life- threatening, dangerous, grim,

Tye marac (*adv*): woefully,

Tye moo moo (*v*): gel,

Tye nono (*adj*): empty, unfilled, blank,

Tye tek (*adj*): thorny, difficult, tricky, problemtic,

Tye tek me nyaŋo ne (*v*): decipher,

Tye weŋ (*adj*): normal, common,

Tye won (*v*): own, possess,

Tyeki (*adj*) complete, finish,

Tyeko (*v*): complete, finish, close, conclude, end,

Tyeko lok (*v*): heal, make good, settle, iron,

Tyelo (*n*): leg,

Tyen (*n*): foot,

Tyen acel (*adj*): asporadical, occasional,

Tyen acel (*adv*): once

Tyen acel acel (*adv*): sporadically, occasionally,

Tyen acel imwaka (*adj*): annual,

Tyen ariyo (*adv*): twice

Tyen ariyo (*n*): twice,

Tyen lela (*n*): pedal,

Tyen lok (*n*): cause, reason, aim, end, purpose, function, point, aim,

Tyen loke peke (*adj*): empty, meaningless,

Tyen madwoŋ (*adj*): frequently, often, regularly, normally, commonly, recurrently, habitually, repeatedly, daily, numerous, many, several, quite a lot,

Tyen mapol (*adj*): several, mumerous, quite a lot,

Tyene (*n*): end, purpose,

Tyene (*n*): stand, rack,

Tyer (*n*): chip, crack, smash,

Tyer (*n*): split, tear,

Tyer oyoto (a*dj*): breakable, fragile, delicate, brittle, frail, precious,

Tyero (*v*): crack,

U

Uc (*adv*): glee,

Udo (*n*): ostrich,

Uganda (*n*): Uganda,

Uke (*adj*): profuse,

Uke (*n*): gush, flood, overflow,

Uko (lok) (*v*): exaggerate,

Um (*n*): nose,

Umo (*adj*): private, concealed,

Umo (*v*): cover, wrap,

Umo kom (*adj*): muffled,

Uno (*adj*): bumpy,

Ur (*adj*): surprised, wonderful, magnificient, amazing, breathtaking, astonishing, fantastic, superb, bewildered, magic, startling,

Ur (*n*): marvel, shock, surprise,

Ur madit (*adj*): astonishing, (*lit*), surprise greatly

Uranac (*n*): Uranus,

Uro (*v*): marvel, shock, stun, surprise, wonder,

W

Wa (kany, iye, kuca) (*adv*): extensively, to a great extent,

Wa (*prep.*): to,

Wa iŋe (*prep.*): beyond,

Wac (*adj*): sour, acid,

Wac kom (*adj*): lazy, indolent,

Wace ko (*adj*), abject, horrible, incredible, dazzling,

Waci (*v*): say, tell,

Waco (*n*): mention,

Waco (*v*): say, tell, voice, relate, state, utter,

Waco gi ma bi time (*v*): foretell,

Waco gi ma tye ka bino i anyim (*v*): predict,

Waco Ka maleŋ (*adj*): express,

Waco ka maleŋ (*v*): rule, declare, affirm,

Waco kit me (*v*): direct, order,

Waco kit me timo ne (*v*): dictate,

Waco lok i wic (*adj*): warning,

Waco lok i wic (*n*): reproach, criticism,

Waco lok i wic (*v*): scold, tell off, warn,

Waco lok iwic (*n*): caution, warning,

Waco lok marac (*v*): swear,

Waco ni (*v*): claim,

Wacon (*prep.*): since,

Wake (*adj*): proud,

Wake (*n*): boast, pride,

Wake (*v*): brag, boast,

Walo (*adj*): boiling, sizzling,

Walo (*n*): boil,

Walo (*v*): boil, shimmer,

Walo doki tul tul (*adj*): hot, boiling,

Wan (*n*): harm,

Wan (*pron.*): we, us,

Wan ki komwa (*pron.*): ourselves,

Wano (*adj*): hurtful, dangerous, hazardous, risky, perilous, precarious, harmful, damaging, injurious,

Wano (*v*): harm, hurt, ail, injure,

Wano dano (*adj*): harmful,

Wano ko (*adj*): harmless,

Wanya (*adj*) craving, desire,

Wanyo (*v*): bare,

Waŋ (*n*): burn,

Waŋ (*n*): eye, face,

Waŋ (*n*): face, countenance,

Waŋ boŋo (mu goyo ki pac) (*n*): fold,

Waŋ boro mucero acel nio wa aboŋwen matitino (*n*): millilitre

Waŋ boro mucero apar matitino (*n*): centilitre

Waŋ boro mucero elip acel matitino (*n*): kilo litre,

Waŋ boro mucero mia acel matitino (*n*): litre

Waŋ boro piny mucero acel nio wa aboŋwen matitino (*n*): millimetre

Waŋ boro piny mucero apar matitino (*n*): centimetre

Waŋ boro piny mucero elip acel matitino (*n*): kilometre,

Waŋ boro piny mucero mia acel matitino (*n*): metre

Waŋ caa (*adj*): punctual,

Waŋ doki pilpil (*adj*) fiery,

Waŋ kor me lobo (Man dok yo iwaŋ kor ma gitamo atama ma opoko i lobo yo ibut lobo ki yo wok ceŋ doki kibut lobo ki yo poto ceŋ) (*adj*): equatorial

Waŋ lit (*n*): eye disease,

Waŋ ma twolo (*n*): alert,

Waŋ maleŋ (*adj*): sober,

Waŋ matwolo (*adj*): alert,

Waŋ pek piny mucero acel nio wa aboŋwen matitino (*n*): milligram

Waŋ pek piny mucero apar matitino (*n*): centigram,

Waŋ pek piny mucero elip acel matitino (*n*): kilogram,

Waŋ pek piny mucero mia acel matitino (*n*): gram

Waŋ pek piny mucero million acel matitino (*n*): tone,

Waŋ romo (*adj*): joint,

Waŋ tal malii (*adj*): line,

Waŋe aduno (*adj*): chubby,

Waŋe leŋ (*adj*): generous, kind, liberal, bighearted, openhanded, munificient, giving, charitable,

Waŋe omino woko (*adj*): serious, heavy,

Waŋe opoto i kome (*adj*): sparkling,

Waŋe yo (*adj*): deadpan, blank, straight –faced, pokerfaced,

Waŋo (*v*): burn, fire,

Waŋo binyi binyi (*v*): scorch,

Waŋo ne binyi binyi (*v*): singe, scorch,

Waŋo riŋo (ceya) (*v*): grill,

War (*n*): shoe,

Waraga (*n*): mail, letters, note, paper,

Waraga acoya (*n*): form, document,

Waraga awila magi moko ki odok i okom waraga acwala (*n*): stamp,

Waraga magi wilo awila doki gi mwono ki odok ikom Baca (*n*): stamp,

Waraga me lok aŋeya (*n*): press, newspaper,

Waraga me niyee (*n*): permit, license,

Waraga me wot (*n*): pass, permit, passage,

Wat (*n*): relative,

Waya (*adj*): wiry,

Wayo (*n*): untie,

Wegi gaŋ (*adj*): native, aboriginal, home –grown, local, original, indigenous,

Wegi paco (*adj*): native, aboriginal, home –grown, local, original, indigenous,

Wegi tim (*adj*): native, aboriginal, home –grown, local, original, indigenous,

Wego (*n*): dad, father,

Weki (*conj.*): so as, so that,

Weko (*adj*): deserted, left, abandoned, determined,

Weko (*conj.*): so that,

Weko (nyom,) (*v*): dump,

Weko (*v*): cause, let, gets,

Weko (*v*): desert, evacuate, quit, give up, drop, let fall,

Weko (*v*): excuse, exempt,

Weko (*v*): release,

Weko mutukari (*v*): park,

Weko obedi (*v*): omit, neglect,

Wel (*adj*): prize, value, valuable,

Wel (*n*): value, cost, price,

Wel (*n*): damage, cost,

Wel (*n*): list,

Wel (*n*): mark, score,

Wel (*n*): number,

Wel cene acula (*n*): bill, expense,

Wel cene magi coyo i waraga (*n*): check,

Wel cene magi deno (*n*): principle,

Wel ma ka gi poko ki ariyo doŋ acel (*adj*): odd,

Wel ma kot omoko (*n, leg.*): lump sump,

Wel ma owilo ki wil (*adj*): outlay, expend,

Wel ma pe tye makulu (*n*): fraction

Wel madit ki bot jero (*adj*): positive,

Wel mapoko kome ki acel keken (*adj*): prime,

Wel matidi ki bot jero (*adj*): negative,

Wel mudoŋ (*adj*): outstanding,

Wel mugoyo (*n*): quote, estimate,

Wel wil (*adj*): expenses,

Wele malo (*adj*): opulent, luxurious, wealthy,

Wele tek (*adj*): precious, costly, expensive, luxurious, opulent, pricey,

Wele weŋ (*adj*): gross,

Wele yot (*adj*): cheap,

Weli (*n*): lump,

Welo (*adj*): strange,

Weŋ (*adj*) all, unanimous, grand, all-inclusive, absolute, complete, total, both, entire, every, general, universal, all-purposes, wide-ranging, broad, common, broad-spectrum, stark, sheer, utter,

Weŋ (*adv*): totally,

Weŋ (*pron.*): all,

Weŋ ko (*adj*): exclusive, partial,

Weŋe (*prep.*): around, all over,

Wer (ki dwan maliu) (*v*): yodel,

Wer (*n*): chant, song, rhyme,

Were (*n*): excuse,

Were ko (*adj*): inevitable,

Were kwe (*adj*): inevitable,

Werewere (*adj*): plastic,

Wero (*v*): sing, chant,

Wero awera (pwony) (*v*): drill,

Wero i wic (*v*): practice, rehearse,

Wero i wic (*v*): memorize, recite,

Wero ki dwan maliu (*v*): yodel,

Weyo (*v*): avoid,

Wi ati (*adj*): early,

Wi cam ma patpat (*n*): diet,

Wi kala ma patpat (*adj*): multicoloured,

Wi lobiko (*n*): point,

Wi lok (*n*): matter, subject, point, headland,

Wi pwony (*n*): matter, subject,

Wic (*n*): head,

Wic maloke atata (*adj*) whimsical,

Wil (*n*): buy, purchase,

Wil ko(*adj*): memorable, unforgettable, classic,

Wilawila (*adj*): draft,

Wilo (*v*): buy, shop,

Wilo ki iwigi (*v*): forget,

Winy (*adj*): obedient,

Winy (*n*): contact,

Winy (*n*): feel, hearing, sense, feeling,

Winy mukwoŋo (*n, leg.*): first instance,

Winye (*n*) tie, connection,

Winye (*v*): relate, interact,

Winye tye (*n*): harmony,

Winyo (*n*): bird,

Winyo (*v*): favour,

Winyo (*v*): feel, sense,

Winyo (*v*): hear, listen,

Winyo (*v*): obey,

Winyo dog (*v*):   submit,

Winyo kom maber (*v*): enjoy,

Winyo kop pa Luŋol kop adek nyo madwoŋ (*n*): full court,

Winyo laro lok (*n, leg.*): proceeding,

Winyo lok (*adj*): submissive, obedient,

Winyo lok (*n, leg.*): hearing,

Winyo lok ko (*adj*): disloyal,

Winyo maber (*adj*): comfortable, abounding, affluent, rich, well –off, well-to-do, flourishing, thriving, successful, booming, relieved,

Winyo maber ko (*adj*): uncomfortable,

Winyo madiŋ (*adj*): uncomfortable, unhealthy, terrible,

Wire (*adj*): revolving, rotating,

Wire (*n*): cycle,

Wire (pa caa) (*n*): tick,

Wire (*v*): explore,

Wire (*v*): spin,

Wire doki wirwir (*v*): whirl,

Wire guluc guluc (*v*): wallow,

Wire ki iwiye (*v*): hover,

Wire mot (*v*): poke,

Wire pa ciŋ (*n*): flourish,

Wiro (*adj*): circular, circulated

Wiro (*n*): turn,

Wiro ciŋ (*n*): wave, waving,

Wiro ki moo (*v*): grease, lubricate,

Wiro wic (*v*): nod, lose concentration, dizzy,

Wito (*v*): throw, fling, pelt,

Wito ga (*n*): throw,

Wito ga ma cwiny mito ko (*v*): dump,

Wito gumi (*n*): jab,

Wiye (*n*): face, surface,

Wiye madoŋo doŋo (*n*): point, headland,

Wiye ne atata (*adj*): zany,

Wiye odiŋ (*adj*): dull,

Wiye opuro matar (*adj*): scaly,

Wiye rac (*adj*): kooky,

Wiye tek (*adj*): extroverted,

Wiye tiyo ko (*adj*): kook,

Wiye wil kala (*adv*): absentmindedly

Wiye wiye (*adj*): brief, superficial, on the surface, surface,

Wiye wiye (doro ga, coc) (*n*): sketch,

Wiye yot (*adj*): apt, gullible,

Wiye yot (*adj*): quick –witted, sharp, intelligent,

Wod *(n)*: son,

Wok (*n*): gap in the teeth,

Wok (*v*): reach,

Wok ceŋ (*n*): East,

Woko (*adv*): outdoors,

Woko doŋ (*adv*): already,

Wolo (*v*): infect,

Won (gaŋ, twero,) (*adj*): responsible,

Won kom (*n*): chairperson,

Won twero (*adj*): executive, administrator,

Won twero (*adj*): responsible,

Woŋ (*adv*): away, far, distant, long way,

Woŋ (*prep.*): outside, beyond,

Woo (*adj*): noisy, deafening, vociferous, loud,

Woo (calo me gaŋ tic) (*adj*): bustling,

Woo (*n*): shout, noise, row, rant,

Woo (*v*): shout,

Woo doki war war (*adj*): deafening,

Woo iwic (*adj*): Jeered,

Woo iwic (*v*): rant,

Woo makwak (*adj*): deafening, noisy,

Woo matek (*adj*): loud,

Woo wau wau kilok (*n*): babble,

Wor (*adj*): decent, decent, orderly, polite,

Woro (*adj*): adored, esteemed, idolized, respectful,

Woro (*adj*): greedy,

Woro (*n*): respect,

Woro (oddo gilac) (*n*): toast,

Wot (*n*): hop, journey,

Wot (*n*): walk,

Wot (*v*): walk,

Wot ŋinaŋina (*adj*): lumbering,

Wota awota (*adj*): flaky, coming off, detaching, peeling,

Woto (*v*): remove, take away,

Woto (*v*): walk,

Woto cwiny (*v*): exempt, ignore, pay no attention to,

Woto cwiny (*v*): spare, do without,

Woto cwiny dano (*adj*): uninteresting, dull,

Woto cwiny ki iye (*v*): igonore,

Woto ikin dano (*v*): mix, socialized,

Woto ki nyate (*v*): strut,

Woto ki ŋuro (*v*): mutter,

Woto ki yeya (*v*): sail,

Woto laboŋ tyene (*v*): wander,

Woto nyutnyut (*v*): wriggle,

Woto ŋina ŋina (*adj*): lumbering,

Wun (*pron.*): you,

Y

Yabo (*v*): enter, input, key in, open, unlock, not closed,

Yabo (*v*): operate, function, activate, run,

Yabo ka maleŋ (*v*) reveal,

Yac (*n*): pregnant,

Yak (*n*): hijack,

Yako (*v*): rob, hijack, mug,

Yamo (*n*): air, tempreture, weather, online,

Yamo ma kodo mot (*adj*): breeze, cool,

Yamo marac (*n*): bad omen, misfortune

Yamo okutu wiye (*adj*): witty,

Yamo tye iwiye (*n*): crazy, mad, silly,

Yaŋ (*adv*): once

Yaŋ con ki con (*adv*): Once upon atime:

Yaŋ pe kany (*adj*): outlandish,

Yaŋo del (*v*): pelt,

Yare (*n*): stretch,

Yaro (*v*): expand, extend, zoom,

Yat (*adj*): medical,

Yat (*n*): medicine, drug,

Yat (*n*): tree,

Yat Acholi (*n*): herbalist,

Yat me gwoko kom (*n*): anti biotic,

Yat me nino (*n*): sleeping pills,

Ye waŋ (*adj*): interesting, attractive, noteworthy, palatable, acceptable, rewarding, well, agreeable,

Ye wele (*v*): yield,

Yec (*n*): tear,

Yeco (*v*): tear, rip,

Yecu (*n*): Jesus,

Yee *(v)*: accept, agree to, acknowledge, admit, allow, believe, concede, consent, permit, face, obey,

Yee (*v*): profess, admit,

Yee (*v*): stipulate,

Yelo (*adj*): yellow

Yelo (dano) (*adj*): disturbing, creepy,

Yelo wi dano (*v*): pester,

Yelo wic (*v*): harass,

Yelo wic (*v*): haunt, trouble, disturb,

Yelyel (*adj*): fluffy,

Yene tek (*adj*): incredible, hard to believe, unbelievable, implausible,

Yeny (*n*): search, find, check, hunt,

Yenyo (*adj*): boiling, steaming, bubbly,

Yenyo (*v*) search, find, look for, seek, check, verify, fish, trace,

Yenyo (*v*): bubble,

Yenyo (*v*): comb, search, poke,

Yenyo (*v*): identify, discover,

Yenyo (*v*): rise,

Yenyo alii (*v*): harass,

Yenyo piny (*v*): inspect, check,

Yeŋe (*adj*): wobbly, shaky, vibrant, bumpy,

Yeŋe (*n*) shake, tremble,

Yeŋe ko (*adj*): steady, stable, abiding, unshakable, unwavering,

Yeŋe lobo lobo (*adj*): wobbly,

Yeŋe lobolobo (*v*): wobble,

Yeŋo (*v*) shake, satisfy, shiver, tremble, rock,

Yeŋo cwiny (*adj*): scared, frightened, terrified, timid, petrified,

Yeŋo cwiny dano (*adj*): frightened, frightening, horrible, scary,

Yeŋo waŋ dano (*adj*): reasonable,

Yeŋo wic (gam lok) (*n*): nod,

Yeŋo wic (*v*): nod,

Yer (*adj*): decision,

Yer (*n*): hair,

Yer (*n*): pick,

Yer (*n*): picking,

Yer ki i kin ga (bako ga) (*n*): draw,

Yer kom mu mwole mapwot (*n*): down,

Yer mapwot (*n*), down, fine hair,

Yer ne mapwot (*adj*): fluffy,

Yer tik (*n*): beard,

Yer waŋ (*n*): eyebrow,

Yere (*adv*): agreeable,

Yere ko (*adj*): unacceptable,

Yero (*v*): pick, choose,

Yesu (*n*): Jesus,

Yet (*adj*): insult, abuse, offense, slur,

Yeto (*v*): offend,

Yeya (*n*): boat,

Yiko (*v*): bury, inter, lay to rest,

Yilo (*adj*): itchy,

Yilo (*v*): itch,

Yilo kom (*n*): itching,

Yir (*adj*): bewitched

Yir (*n*): spell,

Yiro (*v*): enchant,

Yiro yiro (*adj*): smoogy,

Yo (piny) (*prep.*): down, along,

Yo (*prep.*): past,

Yo i (*prep.*): to, toward,

Yo i ŋete tum cel keken (*adv*): unilaterally,

Yo iŋe yeya (*adj*): abaft,

Yo iteŋ (*prep.*): opposite,

Yo me (*adj*): mean,

Yo me (*adj*): medium,

Yo woko (*adj*): outward,

Yoga (*n*): yoga,

Yoge (*n*): tumble, jolt,

Yoge (tol, boŋo) (*n*): fray,

Yoge (*v*): jolt

Yoge (*v*): loosen,

Yogo (peko, teko,) (*v*): lighten,

Yogo (*v*): bumb, tumble,

Yoke ko (*adj*): sure- footed,

Yom (*adj*): soft, fluffy, mushy, tender,

Yom (kwon) (*adj*): tender,

Yom cwiny (*adj*): content, happy, satisfied, pleased, comfortable, impressive, interesting, motivating, jolly, jovial, merry, nice,

Yom cwiny (*n*): delight, relish, happiness,

Yom cwiny ko (*adj*): horrible, unhappy,

Yom cwiny makwak (*adj*): electric,

Yom cwiny pere calo too ko (*adj*): happy-go-lucky,

Yomo cwiny (*adj*) delightful, very pleasing, dazzling, impressive, glittering, amused, amusing, delight, excitable, exciting, fancy, grand, impressive, magnificient, monumental, nice, pleasant,

Yomo cwiny (*adv*): well, admirably,

Yomo cwiny (*v*): delight, rejoice, enchant,

Yomo cwiny (*v*): grip, capture somebody's interest,

Yomo cwiny (*v*): impress, make an impression, please,

Yomo cwiny ko (*adj*): unpleasant,

Yomo cwiny makwak (*adj*): awesome, lovely, splendid, very impressive, maginficient, stupendous,

Yoo (*n*): path, road, way,

Yot (*adj*): cheap, easy, simple, easy, plain, straightforward, uncomplicated, trouble –free, undemanding, unfussy, inexpensive, light,

Yot kom (*adj*): animated, lively, vigorously, sparkling, active, vivacious, dynamic, bubbly, spirited, feisty, lively, energetic, nimble,

Yot kom (*adj*): brisk

Yot kom (*n*): exercise,

Yot kom (pa ŋat ma otii) (*adj*): spry,

Yot me nyaŋo ne (*adj*): clear – cut

Yot wic (*adj*): imaginative,

Yub (*adj*): clear, (*lit.*) party, (*v.*) tidy,

Yub (*adj*): neat, orderly,

Yub (*n*): fix, repair,

Yube (*v*): improve, prepare, get ready,

Yubo (*adj*): fix,

Yubo (*v*): build,

Yubo (*v*): clear, tidy,

Yubo (*v*): dress, adorn,

Yubo (*v*): fix, repair, make, mend,

Yubo (*v*): prepare, make, cook,

Yubo (*v*): produce, make something, manufacture something,

Yubo ayub me gi moni (*v*): produce; organize the making of something,

Yubo kome (*adj*): dapper, neat, elegant, trim, well-dressed, well turned –out, tidy, spruce,

Yubo ot pa winyo (*v*): nest,

Yubo salad (*n*): dressing,

Yubo tyen lok me tic kilok onyo tito nyiŋ gi mo keken (*n*): adverb

Yubo wic (*v*): behave,

Yugi (*n*): rubbish, weed, waste, litter, garbage, dump,

Yuko cwiny (*v*): inspire, motivate,

Ywac (*n*): draw, attraction,

Ywac (*n*): draw, pull, drag,

Ywac (*n*): sniff,

Ywayo (*v*): attract, draw,

Ywayo (*v*): drag, haul, draw, pull out, pull,

Ywayo (*v*): sniff,

Ywayo (*v*): tow,

Ywayo lok (*adj*): snoopy,

Ywe (*adj*): rest, relieved,

Ywe (*n*): pause, break,

Ywe (*v*): breathe, respire,

Ywe doki pupu (*v*): pant,

Ywe mapek (*n*): sigh,

Ywe mapek (*v*): sigh, snort,

Ywec (*n*): stroke,

Ywek (a (*adj*): famous,

Yweka (*n*): fame,

Yweka (*n*): name, celebrity,

Yweyo (ki bakum): vaccum,

Yweyo (kom) (*v*): stroke,

Yweyo (kom) (*v*): pet,

Yweyo (kom) (*v*): rub,

Yweyo (*n*): break, pause, vacation, rest,

Yweyo (*n*): nap,

Yweyo (*v*): nap,

Ywic (*adj*): slight,

Ywic (*n*): slip,

Ywic (*v*): slip, slide,

Ywic ko (*adj*): sure –footed,

Ywire (*v*): skate, glide, slip, slide,

Ywire i wi pee (*v*): ski,

Ywire ki ciketbod (*v*): skateboard,